Investigate the Possibilities

Elementary Physical Science

Forces & Motion

From High-speed Jets to Wind-up Toys

Teacher's Guide

Tom DeRosa
Carolyn Reeves

Forces & Motion
Teacher's Manual

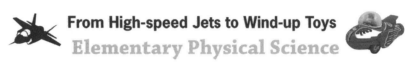

From High-speed Jets to Wind-up Toys
Elementary Physical Science

Tom DeRosa
Carolyn Reeves

First Printing: February 2009

Master Books®
P.O. Box 726
Green Forest, AR 72638

Printed in the United States of America

Cover Design by Diana Bogardus and Terry White
Interior Design by Terry White

ISBN 10: 0-89051-541-7
ISBN 13: 978-0-89051-541-9

All Scripture references are New International Version unless otherwise noted.

Please visit our website for other great titles: www.masterbooks.net

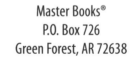

Investigate the Possibilities

TABLE OF CONTENTS

Scientists:
Archimedes (287–212 BC)
Daniel Bernoulli (1700–1782)
Galileo (1564–1642)
Isaac Newton (1642–1727)

INTRODUCTION

The overall goal for each workbook is to include three components: good science, creation apologetics, and Bible references. This goal underlines the rationale for the design of the workbooks.

Science is a great area to teach, because children have a natural curiosity about the world. They want to know why and how things work, what things are made of, and where they came from. The trick is to tap into their curiosity so they want to find answers.

Many elementary-level science lessons begin with definitions and scientific explanations, followed by an activity. A more effective method is to reverse this order and begin with an activity whenever possible. The lessons found in these workbooks begin with an investigation, followed by scientific explanations and opportunities to apply the knowledge to other situations.

In addition to the investigations, there are sections on creation apologetics, written mostly in narrative forms; connections to Bible references; on-your-own challenges; pause and think questions; projects and contests; and historical stories about scientists and engineers. These sections encourage students to think more critically, to put scientific ideas into perspective, to learn more about how science works, to gain some expertise in a few areas, and to become more grounded in their faith in the Bible.

It is not expected that students will do everything suggested in the workbooks. The variety provides students with choices, both in selection of topics and in learning styles. Some students prefer hands-on activities and building things, while others prefer such things as writing, speaking, drama, or artistic expressions. Once some foundational ideas are in place, having choices is a highly motivating incentive for further learning.

Every effort has been made to provide a resource for good science that is accurate and engaging to young people. Most of the investigations were selected from lessons that have been tested and used in our Discovery classrooms. Careful consideration was given to the National Science Education Standards.

The books in this series can be used for a range of grades from 3-8. The National Science Education Standards for levels 5-8 were the basis for much of the content, although K-4 standards were also considered. However, the built-in flexibility allows younger students to do many of the investigations, provided they have good reading and math skills. Older students would be expected to do more independent research and activities.

We feel it is best to leave grading up to the discretion of the teacher. However, for those who are not sure what would be a fair way to assess student work, the following is a suggestion. 1. Completion of 20 activities with write-up of observations — 30 percent. 2. Completion of What Did You Learn Questions + paper and pencil quizzes — 35 percent. 3. Projects, Contests, and Dig Deeper — 35 percent.

The teacher must set the standards for the amount of work to be completed. The basic lessons will provide a solid foundation for each unit, but additional research and activities are a part of the learning strategy. The number of required projects should depend on the age, maturity, and grade level of the students. All students should choose and complete at least one project each week or 20 per semester. Fifth and sixth graders should complete 25 projects per semester. A minimum guide for seventh and eighth graders would be 30 projects. The projects can be chosen from "Dig Deeper" ideas or from any of the other projects and features. Additional projects would give extra accredits. By all means, allow students to pursue their own interests and design their own research projects, as long as you approve first. Encourage older students to do the more difficult projects.

Student should record the date in which each investigation, each Dig Deeper project, and any other work is completed. Use the Table of Contents in the Student Manual to keep this record. You may or may not wish to assign a grade for total points. But a fair evaluation would be three levels, such as: minimum points, more than required, and super work. Remember, the teacher sets the standards for evaluating the work.

Ideally, if students miss a lab, they should find time to make it up. When this is not practical, make sure they understand the questions at the end of the lesson and have them do one of the "Dig Deeper" projects or another project.

You should be able to complete most of the 20 activities in a semester. Suppose you are on an 18-week time frame with science labs held once a week for two or three hours. Most investigations can be completed in an hour or less. Some of the shorter activities can be done on the same day or you may choose to do a teacher demonstration of a couple of the labs. It is suggested that at least five hours a week be allotted to the investigations, contests, sharing of student projects, discussion of "What Have You Learned" questions, and research time. More time may be needed for some of the research and projects.

Most of the equipment can be obtained locally. You may want to order a few things, such as a graduated cylinder and a spring force measure. You may want to start collecting supplies, such as safety glasses, pulleys, C-clamps, metric rulers (with cm divided into tenths), sandpaper, heavy string, plastic film canisters, paper clips, plastic tubing, balloons, dowels, screwdrivers, and screws.

Note that the scientists introduced in this book, along with their life span, are listed with the Table of Contents. A useful tool is to make a timeline. A long chart about 30 cm high and 3 to 5 meters long allows the chart to be divided into equal 100-year intervals beginning with 2000 B.C. and continuing through 2010 A.D. As each new scientist is introduced, a strip of paper can be taped to the chart showing the life span of the scientist, the name of the person, and the person's accomplishments. It will be easy to see which scientists were contemporaries, as well as to see how scientific and technical knowledge is increasing. Some engineers will also be highlighted.

Wind-up Walking Toys
Speed, Time, and Distance

Think about This

Many people still consider "Bullet" Bob Hayes to be the world's fastest runner. In the 1964 Tokyo Olympics, he was part of a 4 X 100 relay race. He was already running when he took the baton. He completed his 100 meters of the relay in 8.6 seconds. He also ran the 100-meter dash in 10.05 seconds. In this race, he started from a still position. Four years later at the Mexico City Olympics, James Hines ran an official time in the 100-meter dash that was less than 10.0 seconds for the first time ever. His record stood for several more years, but Bullet Bob's relay race time will be a hard record to break.

These very fast runners were moving an average of about ten meters every second. Use a meter stick to mark off ten meters and make a prediction of how many meters you think you could run each second. Would you like to be able to figure out how many meters you can run in one second?

We can calculate the speed of a moving object by testing wind-up toys. How far a wind-up toy moves can be measured with a ruler. How long it takes the toy to move a certain distance can be measured with a watch. These two numbers can be used to calculate its speed.

The Investigative Problems

How can we determine the speed and motion of a wind-up walking toy?
How can this be shown on a graph?

6

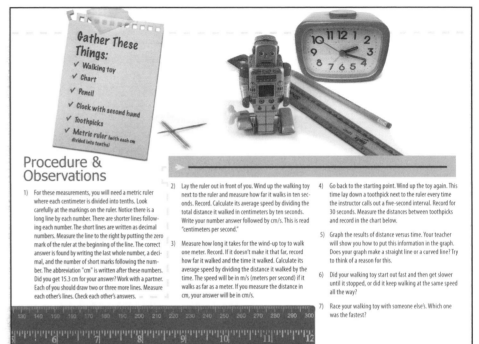

Gather These Things:
✓ Walking toy
✓ Chart
✓ Pencil
✓ Clock with second hand
✓ Toothpicks
✓ Metric ruler (with each cm divided into tenths)

Procedure & Observations

1) For these measurements, you will need a metric ruler where each centimeter is divided into tenths. Look carefully at the markings on the ruler. Notice there is a long line by each number. There are shorter lines following each number. The short lines are written as decimal numbers. Measure the line to the right by putting the zero mark of the ruler at the beginning of the line. The correct answer is found by writing the last whole number, a decimal, and the number of short marks following the number. The abbreviation "cm" is written after these numbers. Did you get 15.3 cm for your answer? Work with a partner. Each of you should draw two or three more lines. Measure each other's lines. Check each other's answers.

2) Lay the ruler out in front of you. Wind up the walking toy next to the ruler and measure how far it walks in ten seconds. Record. Calculate its average speed by dividing the total distance it walked in centimeters by ten seconds. Write your number answer followed by cm/s. This is read "centimeters per second."

3) Measure how long it takes for the wind-up toy to walk one meter. Record. If it doesn't make it that far, record how far it walked and the time it walked. Calculate its average speed by dividing the distance it walked by the time. The speed will be in m/s (meters per second) if it walks as far as a meter. If you measure the distance in cm, your answer will be in cm/s.

4) Go back to the starting point. Wind up the toy again. This time lay down a toothpick next to the ruler every time the instructor calls out a five-second interval. Record for 30 seconds. Measure the distances between toothpicks and record in the chart below.

5) Graph the results of distance versus time. Your teacher will show you how to put this information in the graph. Does your graph make a straight line or a curved line? Try to think of a reason for this.

6) Did your walking toy start out fast and then get slower until it stopped, or did it keep walking at the same speed all the way?

7) Race your walking toy with someone else's. Which one was the fastest?

7

OBJECTIVES

Investigation #1 shows how motion of an object can be described by its speed, time in motion, distance, and direction. Students learn to accurately use a metric ruler. They measure time elapsed and distance traveled for a walking toy. They use this information to make a graph and to calculate speed. Motion can be measured and represented on a graph.

NOTE

Measurement is such a basic scientific skill that all students should master how to use a ruler. The measurement of the line should be exact to the nearest tenth of a centimeter. Include exact length of the line students measure. Be sure to give them opportunities to measure other items if some students seem uncertain. For example, have them estimate and measure some things at their workstations, such as the height of the pages in their book in centimeters or the height of a particular letter or number. Measurements smaller than 1 cm should be written as 0.X cm. A letter might be 0.2 cm in height. Remind students that all scientific measurements are done in metric units. Also, be sure that every measurement includes a number and a unit (cm, m, g, etc.). Generally, a number alone is not a correct answer — an answer must include both a number and a unit.

In making graphs, students should identify evenly spaced lines. Use 0 through 30 seconds for the bottom horizontal axis. For the distance on the vertical axis, you may need to go from 0 to 30 cm, 0 to 60 cm, or 0 to 120 cm, depending on how far they walked.

The Science Stuff

The motion of an object can be described by changes in its position, by its direction, and by its speed. Speed can be calculated by measuring the distance an object moves and the time it takes to move that distance. Divide the distance by the time to get the speed.

The distance traveled equals the object's speed multiplied by the time traveled. The same units of time must be used. For example, if a toy travels 50 cm/minute and it travels for a total of two minutes, it has traveled a total of 100 cm. The calculations would be 50 cm/min X 2 min = 100 cm. Minutes would cancel out, leaving cm as part of your answer.

Different aspects of motion can be shown on a graph. If the speed of the walking toy stayed the same, the graph line will be straight, but if your walking toy slowed down, the graph line will be a curve. Remember, the source of energy for walking toys is a wind-up spring. A tight spring may provide more energy than a loose spring.

Scientific measurements are taken in metric units. The correct abbreviation for centimeter is cm; for meter, it is m. The correct abbreviation for centimeters per second is cm/s; for meters per second, m/s.

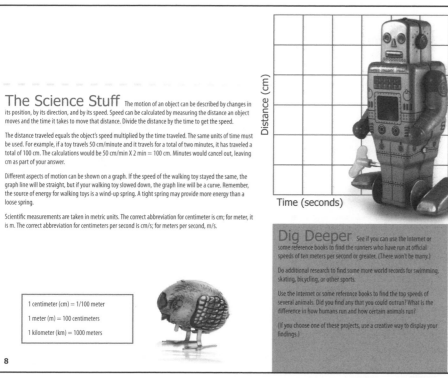

Distance (cm) / Time (seconds)

1 centimeter (cm) = 1/100 meter
1 meter (m) = 100 centimeters
1 kilometer (km) = 1000 meters

Dig Deeper

See if you can use the Internet or some reference books to find the runners who have run at official speeds of ten meters per second or greater. (There won't be many.)

Do additional research to find some more world records for swimming, skating, bicycling, or other sports.

Use the Internet or some reference books to find the top speeds of several animals. Did you find any that you could outrun? What is the difference in how humans run and how certain animals run?

(If you choose one of these projects, use a creative way to display your findings.)

8

Making Connections

Sometimes a highway patrol officer will stop a car for speeding, and the driver will insist that the car was traveling within the speed limit. Is it possible that a car's speedometer is not accurate? Mile markers along the highway and a watch can tell if your car's speedometer is accurate. To do a test, have the driver hold the car's speed at 60 miles/hour. Start timing with a watch that has a second hand as the car reaches a mile marker. Stop timing as the car reaches the next mile marker. The speedometer is accurate if the car travels one mile in 60 seconds. One mile/minute is the same as 60 miles/hour. You can also calculate the speed of your car by dividing the distance of one mile by the time it takes the car to travel from one mile marker to another.

Suppose you are traveling in a car with the cruise control set at 65 miles per hour and your driver drives for two hours without stopping. Multiply the speed by two hours to see how many miles you have traveled in two hours, as: 65 mi/hr X 2 hr = 130 miles.

What Did You Learn?

1) What two things do you need to know in order to calculate speed?

2) What is the formula for calculating speed?

3) How would a line graph of the speed of a runner look when the runner goes slower and slower? Or faster and faster? Or maintains the same speed?

4) What are three ways in which motion can be described?

5) If you are riding in a car that is traveling at 60 miles per hour and you travel for three hours, how far have you traveled?

6) Suppose an object is traveling at a supersonic speed of 800 m/s. Write this speed using all words and no symbols.

7) Calculate the speed of an animal that ran 50 meters in 10 seconds. Write the number answer with the correct unit symbols.

8) What is the source of energy for the walking toys you used for this activity?

9

Show students how to find and mark the intersection of two numbers on the graph. For example, if a toy walks 5 centimeters in 5 seconds, find where 5 cm intersects with 5 sec and put a dot there. If the toy walks 9 cm in 10 sec, estimate the 9 cm line and put a dot where these two lines intersect. When you finish, connect the dots. If the line curves down, that means the toy slowed down; a line that curves up means the toy sped up; a straight line means the toy walked at the same speed.

WHAT DID YOU LEARN?

1. What two things do you need to know in order to calculate speed? *Time and distance*

2. What is the formula for calculating speed? *Speed = distance/time*

3. How would a line graph of the speed of a runner look when the runner goes slower and slower? *It would curve down.* Or faster and faster? *It would curve up.* Or maintains the same speed? *It would be a straight line.*

4. What are three ways in which motion can be described? *By change of position, direction, and speed.*

5. If you are riding in a car that is traveling at 60 miles per hour, and you travel for 3 hours, how far have you traveled? *60 mi/hr X 3 hr = 180 miles.*

6. Suppose an object is traveling at a supersonic speed of 800 m/s. Write this speed using all words and no symbols. *Eight hundred meters per second.*

7. Calculate the speed of an animal that ran 50 meters in 10 seconds. Write the number answer with the correct unit symbols. *50 meters divided by 10 seconds = 5 m/s*

8. What is the source of energy for the walking toys you used for this activity? *A wind-up spring.*

Which Way Did It Go?
Is There More Than One Interpretation for the Same Facts?

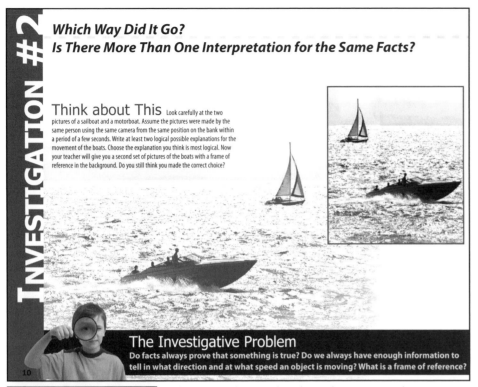

Think about This Look carefully at the two pictures of a sailboat and a motorboat. Assume the pictures were made by the same person using the same camera from the same position on the bank within a period of a few seconds. Write at least two logical possible explanations for the movement of the boats. Choose the explanation you think is most logical. Now your teacher will give you a second set of pictures of the boats with a frame of reference in the background. Do you still think you made the correct choice?

The Investigative Problem
Do facts always prove that something is true? Do we always have enough information to tell in what direction and at what speed an object is moving? What is a frame of reference?

10

Gather These Things:
- ✓ Toy wagon
- ✓ Walking toy
- ✓ Long, smooth board
- ✓ Broom handle or other vertical bar

Procedure & Observations
Do this with a partner, and take turns being the viewer. Place a flat board on a toy wagon. Place a broom handle in a vertical position behind the wagon. Pull the wagon at a slow, steady pace. Place a wind-up walking toy at one end of the board, so that it walks in the opposite direction the wagon is being pulled. Tell your partner the broom handle is the frame of reference. Your partner should focus on the positions of the broom handle and the walking toy when you call start (when you start the walking toy) and when you call stop (when the walking toy is near the end of the board). Find the meaning of "frame of reference."

Between the time you started and stopped your observations, did the walking toy change positions relative to the broom handle? Make a diagram of the walking toy and the frame of reference (broom handle) when you began observing. Make another diagram of these things at the end of your observations. Don't be concerned about the position of the wagon.

Imagine that you are on the board behind the walking toy and you can't see any other objects. How would the toy appear to you to be moving?

The Science Stuff
A frame of reference is something you assume is not moving. You can compare the movement of other objects to your frame of reference and determine changes in position, direction, and speed. Having a frame of reference allowed you to determine which boat in the pictures was moving. It also allowed you to determine how the walking toy was moving relative to the stationary objects in the room.

An important concept illustrated by this activity is that there is often more than one way to explain a set of facts and observations. How movement is interpreted depends on one's point of view and location. It is possible to have different interpretations of how objects are moving if their movement is compared to different frames of reference.

You can see why it took early scientists so long to figure out how the sun, moon, earth, planets, and stars were moving. Everything is moving, and there are no fixed frames of reference anywhere.

11

OBJECTIVES

All motion is shown to be relative, because everything is in motion. The earth is spinning on its axis, the earth is moving around the sun, and the sun is moving around the Milky Way Galaxy. Students are also reminded that there is more than one way to explain a set of facts.

NOTE

The initial activity for this lesson calls for the teacher to show the students two sequential pictures of a sailboat and a motorboat in a body of water where no stationary background can be seen. Ask if anyone can tell which boat is moving. Ask what are some possible explanations for what happened. The sequence of the pictures indicates that either the sailboat moved, the motorboat moved, or they both moved. You may refer to the drawings in the book or redraw the two pictures of the sailboat and the motorboat on a large sheet of art paper.

Later, show another set of these same pictures of the boats, but with a frame of reference in the background. If you have drawings on art paper, simply add some land in the background with a tree above the sailboat in both pictures, as in these drawings:

With the tree as a frame of reference that doesn't move, it will be obvious which boat is moving.

You can help students grasp the concept of being on a moving earth by helping them to remember times they were in a moving vehicle (airplane, train, bus, or car) moving smoothly at a constant speed and direction. Under those conditions, it would be hard to realize they were moving at all unless they looked outside and saw trees, buildings, and other stationary objects that would act as frames of reference.

Photos for THINK ABOUT THIS

Photo 1

Photo 2

NARRATIVE: Same Set of Facts, Different Explanations

"Hey, Dad, what kind of scientist studies about dinosaurs and fossils?" Joey asked.

"That would be a paleontologist, son," Dr. Houston replied.

"I think I'd like to be a paleontologist some day and collect more fossils and figure out where they all came from," Joey said. "Do you remember the book I found at the library on fossils? It said the first fossils were formed millions and millions of years ago and evolved from a little living thing that only had one cell."

"Yes, that was the book that also said evolution from a one-cell organism was a fact, wasn't it?" In spite of Dr. Houston's scientific background, he believed that all living things are the result of special creation rather than evolution from a common ancestor.

"When I become a paleontologist, I'll do experiments and prove that evolution isn't true," Joey said with confidence.

"I'm afraid there are two problems with that. First of all, science isn't about proving things. It's about finding the most logical explanation that agrees with the facts and observations. Your fossils are facts, but the explanation for where they came from is not a fact."

"The second thing," Dr. Houston continued, "is that paleontologists are not really experimental scientists like me. They are historical scientists, trying to figure out what happened in the past without actually observing the events. They are like detectives looking for clues that were left behind."

"That's okay," Joey said. "I'd like being a detective."

"You know that both detectives and paleontologists run into the problem that the same evidence can often be explained in more than one way. When this happens, scientists may disagree about which explanation is best; which one best agrees with the facts."

Dr. Houston began flipping through a stack of papers until he found the one he was looking for. "I found this illustration the other day to show you. It's a fictional story about a drawing that was found on the wall of a very old buried building. According to the story, this was such an important discovery that scientists were brought in from all over the world to analyze it and study it. The top of the picture looks like tree branches. Toward the bottom of the drawing, there's not much left, but the scientists set to work to reconstruct the drawing."

"Why don't you see if you can figure out what the drawing might have looked like to start with?" Dr. Houston continued.

Joey set to work filling in the gaps. "Okay, I'm through," Joey finally said as he compared his drawing of three trees to what the other students had drawn. He noticed that some had drawn three trees and some had drawn one tree.

"Think of the partial drawing you started with as scientific evidence and facts, and think of the lines you filled in as explanations. Do you see that there is more than one logical explanation or way to reconstruct the drawing, even though everyone began with the same set of facts? Do you see that none of the reconstructed drawings can be called a fact?"

"Yes, sir, that makes sense. And they all look about the same at the top," Joey said. "They are mostly different at the bottom half."

"That's right. The gaps are small at the top, but they get much bigger at the bottom. You weren't absolutely certain about how to reconstruct the top, but you had a high level of certainty."

"Yes, and it became harder to complete the bottom of the drawing."

"Many scientists, especially today's paleontologists, believe that all living things came from one common ancestor. They picture the history of life as a single branching tree of life, where all living things came from the same source. Other scientists say that there is some evidence of branching taking place within similar groups, but not between big groups.

These scientists see the history of life as a forest of trees, where each tree, or living thing, had a separate beginning.

"So, Joey, which picture do you think best represents the history of life — one tree or a forest of trees?"

"I think life began like a forest of trees," Joey added. "Isn't that what Genesis tells us?"

"Absolutely," Dr. Houston said.

*Illustrations are taken from Understanding Science While Believing the Bible by Carolyn Reeves (Memphis, TN: MacBeth Publishers, 2004).

Remains of the original painting   Possible reconstruction #1   Possible reconstruction #2

12

Follow-up Discussions

Your teacher will show you a picture that some textbooks refer to as Darwin's "tree of life." Explain what this picture means. What do you think about books that claim this is a fact? What is the difference in a view of the history of life represented by a single tree of life and a view of the history of life represented by a forest of trees? Remember, Darwin's idea is represented by a single tree of life. The terms monophyletic and polyphyletic are used to express these two views. Which term do you think refers to one common ancestor for all living things? What does Genesis 1 and 2 teach us about the beginning of life?

What is a "scientifically proven fact"?

Making Connections

Many people think of a scientist as someone who discovers facts about nature. This is a big misconception. The reason is that facts are basically things that have been observed or measured in some way. While scientists try to make accurate observations and measurements, facts alone may not tell us very much. Why is this? Because the same set of facts can often be interpreted in different ways.

A scientific theory should never be referred to as a "scientifically proven fact." Sometimes people incorrectly refer to Darwin's theory of evolution from a common ancestor as "the fact of evolution." The only way this could be considered a fact would be to observe all living things evolving from one original form of life.

What Did You Learn?

1) Imagine you are riding a large, flat boat down a river that is moving south at ten miles/hour. You take a toy car and push it north at five miles/hour. If a friend observes the toy car from the riverbank, at what speed and in what direction will it appear to be moving?

2) What is a frame of reference?

3) Why do you need a frame of reference in order to tell how something is moving?

4) Suppose you observe a picture of two boats in a lake, but one of them is not moving. Can you tell for sure which boat was moving unless you have a frame of reference in the picture?

5) Is it possible for the same set of facts to be interpreted in more than one way?

6) Can a scientific theory change into a scientific fact when more evidence is obtained?

Dig Deeper

At one time, many of the world's most intelligent people believed that the sun and stars moved around a stationary earth. What were the facts that the early scientists used as a basis for the theory that the earth was the center of the universe?

What caused scientists to begin to change their minds and accept that the earth, moon, and planets moved around the sun?

What is the Milky Way Galaxy? Do scientists now believe that the sun is moving around the Milky Way Galaxy? Do scientists believe the Milky Way Galaxy is moving through the universe?

13

WHAT DID YOU LEARN?

1. Imagine you are riding a large, flat boat down a river that is moving south at 10 miles/hour. You take a toy car and push it north at 5 miles/hour. If a friend observes the toy car from the riverbank, at what speed and in what direction will it appear to be moving? *The toy car will appear to be moving south at 5 miles/hour.*

2. What is a frame of reference? *The background that you pretend is not moving. (Remember that everything around you is moving, because the earth is spinning on its axis as well as moving around the sun and moving through our galaxy.)*

3. Why do you need a frame of reference in order to tell how something is moving? *You need something with which to compare the moving object to see if its position has changed.*

4. Suppose you observe a picture of two boats in a peaceful lake, but one of them is not moving. Can you tell for sure which boat was moving unless you have a frame of reference in the picture? *Unless there are other clues, such as a wake in the water, you cannot tell which is moving.*

5. Is it possible for the same set of facts to be interpreted in more than one way? *Yes!*

6. Can a scientific theory change into a scientific fact when more evidence is obtained? *No. The level of certainty of the theory may become stronger, but it will still not become a fact unless the theory becomes an observation.*

FOLLOW-UP DISCUSSION

Find a picture of Darwin's tree of life. Explain what this picture means. Naturalistic Darwinists claim that all living things can trace their ancestors back to an original living cell, which evolved into all living things on earth (living and dead). This is often represented by a "tree of life." What is the difference in a view of the history of life represented by a single tree of life and a view of the history of life represented by a forest of trees? Remember, Darwin's idea is represented by a single tree of life. The terms monophyletic and polyphyletic are used to express these two views. A monophyletic view claims that all living things arose from one common ancestor. This is represented by one tree that branches and rebranches. A polyphyletic view claims that there were many original ancestors, which may have changed in size, shape, color, etc., over the years. This is represented by a forest of trees, with each tree showing some branching. What does Genesis 1 and 2 teach us about the beginning of life? Chapters 1 and 2 tell us that God designed and created the heavens and the earth, specifically mentioning the creation of light; time; bodies of water; the sky; dry land; plants; the sun, moon, and stars; water animals; birds; land-dwelling animals; and lastly, humans who were created in the image of God. These chapters agree with a polyphyletic view of the first plants, animals, and humans. What is a "scientifically proven fact"? Facts usually include observations and measurements. Information in data tables is generally considered factual. Hypotheses, theories, and other explanations are not facts.

Investigating Friction

Think about This
Observe a wind-up walking toy trying to walk on a flat, smooth surface that has been oiled. Be sure the toy's feet are smooth and oiled. Why is he having so much trouble walking?

Did you know that without friction, you would have trouble being able to start moving? Did you know that without friction, you would have trouble being able to stop moving?

Procedure & Observations
There are examples of friction all around you. Friction causes your tennis shoes to wear down and may even wear a hole in the soles of your shoes. Make a list of other things around you that have been worn down by friction. Include things that are slightly worn down as well as things that are severely worn down.

Now make another list of ways in which friction is helpful. Remember the example of the walking toy that couldn't walk without enough friction.

Look at a spring force measure. This is a device for measuring the amount of force in a pull. Notice that you get a reading if you pull on it. Your teacher may need to show you how to read the device, because not all spring force measures are the same. Many scientific scales measure the force in units called newtons. (For what scientist do you think this unit was named?) Many scales also show the force in pounds. For what we are investigating, either newtons or pounds may be used.

Place a book on a smooth table. Open the cover of a hardback book. Insert a string and close the cover.

The Investigative Problem
In what ways is friction helpful, and in what ways is friction harmful? How can friction be measured? Does the degree of smoothness of surfaces affect the amount of friction? Is sliding friction greater than rolling friction under the same conditions?

14

Gather These Things:
✓ Heavy string
✓ Spring scale (force measure)
✓ Round pencils
✓ Hardback book (2-4 pounds)

Connect the two ends of the string, so you can pull the book. Attach the spring force measure to the two ends of the string. Hold the force measure and begin to pull on the book. Have a partner read and record the force on the force measure at the moment the book begins to move. Continue to move the book about a meter. Have your partner read and record the force on the force measure when the book is moving steadily. Repeat three times to be sure that you record an accurate force for both readings. Average the readings.

Repeat the experiment with another surface that has a different degree of roughness. Record your results in the data table.

Which required the greater force — starting to move or sliding at a steady rate?

Describe the difference in surface one and surface two. Tell which surface is the roughest.

Was the force of friction greater on surface one or on surface two?

Surface 1	Force to Start	Force to Keep Moving
Trial 1		
Trial 2		
Trial 3		
Average		
Surface 2		
Trial 1		
Trial 2		
Trial 3		
Average		

Now try to reduce friction even more by placing several pencils under the book. Pull the book as it rolls over the pencils. How much force does it take to start the book moving over a rolling surface? How much force does it take to keep it moving over a rolling surface? Which is greater — sliding or rolling friction? (If you pull the book very far, you will need to keep putting pencils ahead of the book.)

Spring force measures are also called spring scales. They have a variety of uses and come in different sizes and models.

Now use your spring force measure to pull some other objects in the room. For each object you test, record the force necessary to start it moving and the force needed to keep it moving at a steady rate. Be creative and write your measurements and observations.

15

OBJECTIVES
Activity 3 shows that friction is both helpful and harmful. Students examine some of the ways that friction helps us and some of the ways friction is bad for us. They understand that the degree of smoothness of two surfaces rubbing together affects the amount of friction that is produced and that sliding friction is greater than rolling friction under the same conditions. Students will use a tool that measures the force needed to move an object. They will take measurements that test different amounts of friction and note the direction in which the object moves. Friction is also affected by the weight of a moving object.

NOTE
The walking toy on an oiled surface makes a good demonstration. Be sure to practice before showing this to the students. A glass, metal, or painted surface will work better than unpainted wood. If the toy's feet are not smooth, they can be painted with a hard fingernail polish and then oiled.

One of the materials recommended for this activity is a spring force measure. If you cannot find scientific scales, you can use fish scales. Be sure to try this out first to see how well it works.

Recalling lots of day-to-day examples of how friction is harmful and how it is helpful will give students an important foundation upon which to base more complex ideas about force and motion.

PAUSE AND THINK
There are many examples of streamlined animals in nature. Many birds and fish are designed to reduce friction as they move through the air or the water. Students should be able to think of several examples.

Acts 4:24 records the prayer of Peter and John just after they had been released from jail and threatened. Spend some time discussing why they were praising God for His creation at this point.

The Science Stuff

Friction is all around you. Friction may create problems, such as causing your tennis shoes and bike tires to wear out. Clothes, shoes, pencils, books, and other items around you are eventually worn down by friction.

On the other hand, we couldn't get by without friction. Just as the walking toy needed friction to walk across the oily surface, we need friction to start moving, to stop moving, to speed up, to slow down, and to change directions. For example, tennis shoes are designed to increase friction. Basketball players need friction to make sudden stops and starts, as well as to change direction and speed. Without friction, pencils wouldn't write and erasers wouldn't erase.

All moving things have friction. When two surfaces rub together, they generate friction. If the surfaces are very rough, they may generate a lot of friction.

Friction is a force, and like all forces, it has a direction and an amount. It pushes or pulls in the opposite direction from which an object is moving. One way friction can be measured is with a spring force measure.

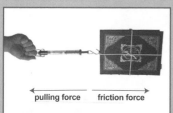

pulling force   friction force

More force is required to start an object moving than to keep it moving. This is partly because the resistance due to friction must be overcome. Another reason is because of inertia, which is a property of all matter. Inertia is the tendency of an object at rest to remain at rest and an object in motion to remain in motion at the same speed and in the same direction. Inertia is a property of matter; it is not a force. We will investigate inertia in more detail in lesson four.

In order for an object to start moving, it must overcome its inertia and the resistance due to friction. To continue moving, it must overcome the resistance due to friction.

Look at the diagram of a student pulling a book. A horizontal arrow shows the pulling force of the student. This force was measured with a spring force measure. The pushing force of friction is shown by another horizontal arrow, going in the opposite direction.

Friction can be affected by the smoothness of two surfaces that are rubbing against each other. The rougher the surfaces, the more friction there is. Rubbing against a smooth surface results in less friction.

Sliding friction is generally greater than rolling friction. Other things, such as the weight of the moving object, can also affect friction.

Making Connections

Try to imagine what would happen if a basketball player wore shoes with hard soles instead of tennis shoes. Tennis shoes with well-designed treads are usually an important investment for basketball players.

Snow tires have extra-thick treads to increase the friction on icy roads. All tires need good treads to have enough friction to drive safely, but on icy roads, extra friction is needed.

Friction is useful in many ways, but it can also be harmful. Friction can cause even the most well-built machines to wear out, so engineers keep looking for ways to reduce friction between the moving parts. Lubricating the moving parts of a machine with oil or graphite can decrease the amount of friction they produce. Lubricants make the surfaces that are rubbing together smoother.

Older models of skates consisted of wheels that turned around a fixed axle. The axles rubbed against the inside of the wheels as they turned, and they had to be oiled to reduce friction. Most skates today have ball bearings or roller bearings between the wheels and the axle to reduce friction. With ball or roller bearings, there is rolling friction instead of sliding

16

Dig Deeper

Engineers who design cars, trucks, boats, airplanes, and rockets look for ways to reduce friction between the vehicle and the air. Making vehicles more streamlined is another way to reduce friction. However, making vehicles too streamlined may create dangerous air turbulences. It also reduces the amount of space inside the vehicle. Collect pictures of the shapes of different vehicles, especially the front ends that hit the air. Try to determine if each vehicle is designed primarily to go faster or to have more space to carry passengers and other items.

SLIPPERY WHEN WET

friction. The axles turn easily and produce little friction.

Another design for reducing friction is the use of air-lubricated machines. These machines are generally expensive, but the amount of friction between the moving parts is extremely small and the machine will last a long time.

Engineers try to reduce friction between the water and boats by making the boat's surfaces smoother. If a boat has a smooth, shiny surface, it can actually go faster and get better gas mileage than a boat with a rough, dull surface.

Have you ever played a game of air hockey? The puck slides easily when the machine is on. It will still slide when it is off, but there is more friction between the puck and the table. When the machine is on, friction is between the puck and a cushion of air — not between the puck and the table.

You can't always do much to reduce friction, except to replace the worn-out parts. Friction may cause the soles of your shoes to become thin or even make holes in them. Tires on your vehicles get worn down by friction and have to be replaced. Friction may cause a pair of blue jeans to get holes in the knees before any other part wears out. Do you see why the frequent motion of bending your knees would result in more friction at the knees of your pants?

Sharks can travel rapidly through the water, because they have very streamlined bodies. Try to find some of the ways in which sharks are designed with streamlined features. Compare a shark's shape to a whale's shape.

What is an example of a machine that uses air lubrication? What are the advantages and disadvantages of this machine?

Have you ever tried to start to run on ice, or slide across the floor in your socks where there wasn't much friction? You should remember it was difficult to start and difficult to stop. Examine a variety of tennis shoes. Notice that the soles of some of the shoes are worn down, while some have deep

treads on the soles. Which shoes do you think would do the best job of helping a basketball player stop, start, speed up, slow down, and change directions? Observe the different kinds of tread patterns on the bottom of the shoes. Make drawings of some of the patterns. Which do you think would be the most effective? List some other items that need friction in order to work properly.

List some ways in which friction affects you every day. Choose one way that friction affects you every day. What did you choose? Keep a record of how friction affects you in this way throughout the day.

Pause & Think

Engineers design vehicles that are streamlined in order to reduce friction with the air. Before there were human engineers, God designed birds to have streamlined features that enable them to fly smoothly through the air without encountering too much friction. For example, birds have no external ears. When a bird is in flight, its legs are held close to its body. From their heads to their tails, birds have an angular, streamlined body, which is made smoother by its feathers. Internally, birds have other features that make them suited for flight. Once, God spoke directly to a man named Job in response to Job's complaints. Job said he had done nothing to deserve all the misfortunes in his life. Part of God's answer to Job was to ask him if hawks took flight by Job's wisdom or if eagles soared at Job's command (Job 39:26–27). God was telling Job that making a bird capable of flying was far beyond Job's wisdom and power, but fully within God's ability. God was also reminding Job to trust His wisdom and His power during those times when he didn't understand what was happening. We know that no man has the wisdom or power to design and create birds. Why should anyone find it logical to think that random natural processes and events could accomplish something that only God can do? When we pause to praise God for the marvels of creation, we are reminded of His wisdom and His great power. Can you name other animals that are designed to reduce friction as they move through air or water?

What Did You Learn?

1) What force causes your tennis shoes to wear out?
2) What force helps you to walk without falling down?
3) In what direction does friction push?
4) Which force is greater if other conditions are the same — rolling friction or sliding friction?
5) Are ball bearings an example of sliding friction or rolling friction?
6) Do cars need friction to start moving or to turn a curve?
7) Under which conditions would there be more friction — moving over rough or smooth surfaces? Moving a heavy or a lightweight object?
8) List some everyday things that create friction where you would consider the friction to be helpful. Next, list some you would consider the friction created to be destructive.
9) What are some ways in which friction can be reduced?
10) What are some things that may affect the amount of friction produced by a moving object?
11) Friction can be measured by what piece of equipment?
12) What property of matter causes an object at rest to remain at rest and an object in motion to remain in motion unless an unbalanced force acts on the object?

17

WHAT DID YOU LEARN?

1. What force causes your tennis shoes to wear out? *friction*

2. What force helps you to walk without falling down? *friction*

3. In what direction does friction push? *opposite to the way an object is moving*

4. Which force is greater if other conditions are the same—rolling friction or sliding friction? *sliding friction*

5. Are ball bearings an example of sliding friction or rolling friction? *rolling friction*

6. Do cars actually need friction to start moving? *yes* Or to turn a curve? *yes*

7. Under which conditions would there be more friction—moving over rough or smooth surfaces? *rough surfaces* Moving a heavy or a lightweight object? *moving a heavy object*

8. List some everyday things that create friction where you would consider the friction to be helpful. *Friction makes your pencil write and your eraser erase. It makes your car stay on the road and enables you to walk and run without falling down, as well as many other things.*

Next, list some you would consider the friction created to be destructive. *Friction makes shoes, clothes, and tires wear out, as well as many other things*

9. What are some ways in which friction can be reduced? *lubricating with oil; lubricating with graphite; use of ball bearings or roller bearings; use of air lubrication; (other ways)*

10. What are some things that may affect the amount of friction produced by a moving object? *the degree of smoothness of a surface, whether the object is sliding or rolling, the weight of the moving object*

11. Friction can be measured by what piece of equipment? *a spring force measure*

12. What property of matter causes an object at rest to remain at rest and an object in motion to remain in motion unless an unbalanced force acts on the object? *inertia*

Friction — Does It Rub You the Wrong Way?

Think about This

Galileo observed that if a ball rolled down an incline, it would continue to roll over a level surface for a distance before it stopped. When he made the surfaces smoother, he found that a ball would travel farther. He continued to find ways to make the surface smoother. Each time, the ball rolled farther before it came to a stop. He finally decided the ball would roll forever in a straight line unless an unbalanced force caused it to stop.

Many years earlier, Aristotle had reasoned that all moving objects have a natural tendency to stop moving. Do you think Galileo agreed with Aristotle?

Procedure & Observations
Part A. What Happens When There Is Less Friction?

Take a smooth board and place a stack of books under one end to make a ramp on a table or the floor. Put the finished side of the carpet strip next to the ramp. Let the toy car roll down the ramp onto the carpet. Measure the distance the car rolls across the carpet. Take three measurements and get an average distance.

Repeat the experiment, letting the car roll across the unfinished side of the carpet strip.

Repeat the experiment again, letting the car roll across a smooth surface (a table, floor, or smooth board).

The Investigative Problem
What is inertia?
Does friction produce heat?

18

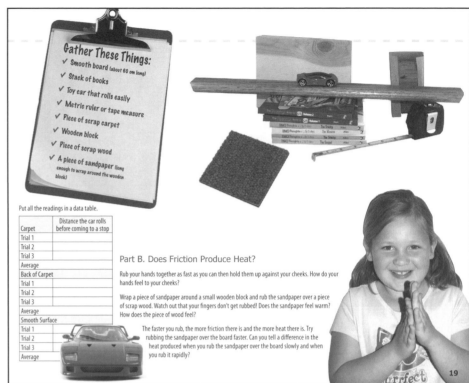

Gather These Things:
- ✓ Smooth board (about 60 cm long)
- ✓ Stack of books
- ✓ Toy car that rolls easily
- ✓ Metric ruler or tape measure
- ✓ Piece of scrap carpet
- ✓ Wooden block
- ✓ Piece of scrap wood
- ✓ A piece of sandpaper (long enough to wrap around the wooden block)

Put all the readings in a data table.

Carpet	Distance the car rolls before coming to a stop
Trial 1	
Trial 2	
Trial 3	
Average	
Back of Carpet	
Trial 1	
Trial 2	
Trial 3	
Average	
Smooth Surface	
Trial 1	
Trial 2	
Trial 3	
Average	

Part B. Does Friction Produce Heat?

Rub your hands together as fast as you can then hold them up against your cheeks. How do your hands feel to your cheeks?

Wrap a piece of sandpaper around a small wooden block and rub the sandpaper over a piece of scrap wood. Watch out that your fingers don't get rubbed! Does the sandpaper feel warm? How does the piece of wood feel?

The faster you rub, the more friction there is and the more heat there is. Try rubbing the sandpaper over the board faster. Can you tell a difference in the heat produced when you rub the sandpaper over the board slowly and when you rub it rapidly?

19

OBJECTIVES

Friction is a force that opposes the motion of a moving object. Ordinarily, friction causes moving objects on earth to slow down and stop; but as friction is reduced, a moving object will continue to move longer. An unbalanced force causes a moving object to stop moving. An object that is not being subjected to a force (such as friction) will continue to move at a constant speed and in a straight line. Friction always produces heat energy, but more heat is produced with rougher surfaces and with faster movement.

NOTE

Galileo and Aristotle are introduced in this lesson as having different ideas about motion. Aristotle thought reasoning and logic was the way to learn about science. He thought it was just natural for moving objects to stop. Galileo (and later Isaac Newton) believed that observations and experiments were the way to do science. They concluded that moving objects stop moving because one or more unbalanced forces, such as friction, cause them to stop. They also came to the conclusion that if there were no unbalanced forces acting on a moving object, it would continue to move forever.

The Science Stuff

The toy car moved farther across the smooth surface than it did across the rougher surfaces.

Imagine that there was no friction acting on the toy car. The car's inertia would still cause it to be harder to start moving than to keep it moving. But did you know that once the car starts moving, its inertia would cause it to keep moving at the same speed and in a straight line? That is, unless it bumped into something or gravity or some other force affected its motion. In other words, it would move forever unless another force caused it to stop!

This is the same principle that Galileo observed as he rolled a ball down an incline and over a smooth surface. He wondered what would happen if friction and other forces were eliminated completely. He predicted that the ball would roll indefinitely.

Later, Isaac Newton continued to study Galileo's ideas. Newton formulated this idea into his first law of motion, which says: If an object is not moving, it has a tendency to remain at rest. If an object is moving, it has a tendency to remain in motion in the same direction and at the same speed unless an unbalanced force acts on it. The property of all matter to behave in this way is known as inertia.

Remember that friction is a force. It pushes in the opposite way an object is moving. Therefore, the more friction there is, the more force there is opposing movement.

The more friction is reduced, the farther a moving object will travel before stopping. Thinking about this will help you understand that a moving object on a straight, level surface with no friction could continue to move indefinitely.

Friction generates heat, which is a form of energy. More heat is produced by rubbing the sandpaper over the board rapidly than by rubbing it slowly. Faster motion produces more friction and more heat. For example, if a meteoroid from space enters the earth's atmosphere, it will fall faster and faster. The friction between the rapidly moving meteor and the air will produce a great deal of heat. This will cause the meteor to catch on fire and burn. If you should see a burning meteor in a night sky, you would probably call it a "shooting star."

Making Connections

Remember some of the ways you have already found in which friction can be reduced. Oil lubrication, graphite, ball bearings, roller bearings, and air lubrication are some of the ways friction can be reduced.

Racing cars, speed boats, and other vehicles designed for speed have smooth, shiny surfaces to reduce friction with the air. Bike racers wear smooth, slick biking pants, and Olympic skaters wear smooth clothes over their heads and bodies. In racing events, reducing friction can be very important. There may only be hundredths of a second that determines the winner.

Before there were matches, people in different cultures learned to use friction as a method of starting fires. You may have seen movies that showed Indians rubbing sticks together to start a fire. Even today, Scouts learn how to start a fire by rapidly rubbing pieces of wood together.

Dig Deeper

Hovercrafts are vehicles that ride on a cushion of air, so that there is no sliding friction between craft and ground or craft and water. You can make a simple model of a hovercraft. There are several methods that are available on the Internet or in the library. See if you can find instructions for a hovercraft using a large, sturdy balloon, a smooth piece of board or cardboard, and a few other items. Test your hovercraft on a smooth surface. As long as air is being forced out of the balloon, your device will slide around easily. Demonstrate your model to other students. You can also make a model to illustrate how ball bearings work. Put little blobs of modeling clay on both ends of your pencil. Find a soup can and a lid that is a little larger than the soup can. Put another blob of clay in the center of the top side of the lid. Push the middle of the pencil into the clay, making sure the pencil is balanced on the lid. Now put several marbles on top of the marbles, place the lid on the marbles, and spin the lid. Take the marbles off and spin the lid again. Compare how well the lid spins with and without the marbles. In which case is there more friction? Demonstrate this to other students.

Spacecraft reenter the earth's atmosphere at very high speeds. How are they designed to withstand the extreme heat that is produced from friction with the air?

On Your Own: The Challenge to Think Like an Engineer

This is a contest to find a way to pull a heavy box from one end of the table to the other, to do it with the least effort, and to do it in two minutes or less. You can put something under it before you start moving it or while you are moving it, but you must pull it all the way without stopping. Your box must be pulled with a string that is attached to a spring force measure. You may only use the materials your teacher provides for this contest.

First try to think of several ways you could reduce friction as you move the box. Think of the activities you have already done about friction. Then make a plan that you think would let you move it with the least effort. Test your idea. Make adjustments if necessary. Your teacher will tell you how much time you have to get ready before the contest.

Each team (or contestant) will attach a spring force measure to the box. The judge will record the sustained moving effort force and the total time it takes. The team who finishes in less than two minutes and moves the box with the lowest sustained effort force will be the winner. In the case of a tie, the team who finishes in the least amount of time will be the winner.

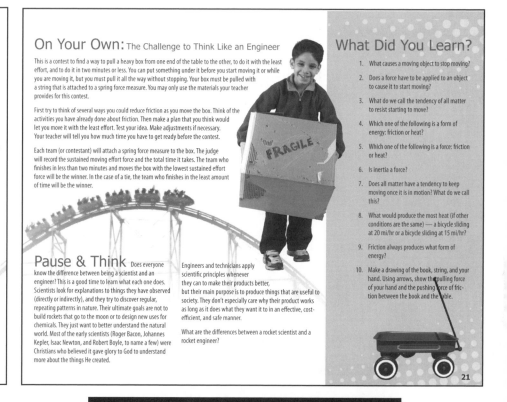

Pause & Think

Does everyone know the difference between being a scientist and an engineer? This is a good time to learn what each one does. Scientists look for explanations to things they have observed (directly or indirectly), and they try to discover regular, repeating patterns in nature. Their ultimate goals are not to build rockets that go to the moon or to design new uses for chemicals. They just want to better understand the natural world. Most of the early scientists (Roger Bacon, Johannes Kepler, Isaac Newton, and Robert Boyle, to name a few) were Christians who believed it gave glory to God to understand more about the things He created.

Engineers and technicians apply scientific principles whenever they can to make their products better, but their main purpose is to produce things that are useful to society. They don't especially care why their product works as long as it does what they want it to in an effective, cost-efficient, and safe manner.

What are the differences between a rocket scientist and a rocket engineer?

What Did You Learn?

1. What causes a moving object to stop moving?
2. Does a force have to be applied to an object to cause it to start moving?
3. What do we call the tendency of all matter to resist starting to move?
4. Which one of the following is a form of energy: friction or heat?
5. Which one of the following is a force: friction or heat?
6. Is inertia a force?
7. Does all matter have a tendency to keep moving once it is in motion? What do we call this?
8. What would produce the most heat (if other conditions are the same) — a bicycle sliding at 20 mi/hr or a bicycle sliding at 15 mi/hr?
9. Friction always produces what form of energy?
10. Make a drawing of the book, string, and your hand. Using arrows, show the pulling force of your hand and the pushing force of friction between the book and the table.

ON YOUR OWN

Provide heavy string and spring force measures. Allow students to choose any two of the following supplies: round pencils, hexagonal pencils, cellophane, various fabrics.

PAUSE AND THINK

Does everyone know the difference in being a scientist and an engineer? This is a good time to learn what each one does.

NOTE

This is a key concept that should build on what students are learning about science. A primary goal of scientists is to look for explanations about things in nature. A rocket scientist, therefore, would try to answer questions about why a rocket works. A rocket engineer would try to build a rocket that is more efficient, faster, safer, or more durable. Engineers apply scientific knowledge whenever they can, but they would be concerned about why a rocket works only if it helped them build a better rocket. (Scientists also look for repeating patterns in nature.)

WHAT DID YOU LEARN?

1. What causes a moving object to stop moving? *An unbalanced force.*
2. Does a force have to be applied to an object to cause it to start moving? *Yes.*
3. What do we call the tendency of all matter to resist starting to move? *Inertia.*
4. Which one of the following is a form of energy: friction or heat? *Heat.*
5. Which one of the following is a force: friction or heat? *Friction.*
6. Is inertia a force? *No. (It is a property of all matter.)*
7. Does all matter have a tendency to keep moving once it is in motion? *Yes.* What do we call this? *Inertia.*
8. What would produce the most heat (if other condition are the same) — a bicycle sliding at 20 mi/hr or a bicycle sliding at 15 mi/hr? *A bicycle sliding at 20 mi/hr.*
9. Friction always produces what form of energy? *Heat.*
10. Make a drawing of the book, string, and your hand. Using arrows, show the pulling force of your hand and the pushing force of friction between the book and the table.

That's Heavy, Dude
Air Pressure

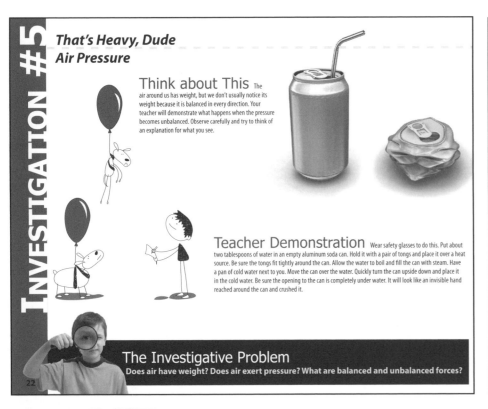

Think about This
The air around us has weight, but we don't usually notice its weight because it is balanced in every direction. Your teacher will demonstrate what happens when the pressure becomes unbalanced. Observe carefully and try to think of an explanation for what you see.

Teacher Demonstration
Wear safety glasses to do this. Put about two tablespoons of water in an empty aluminum soda can. Hold it with a pair of tongs and place it over a heat source. Be sure the tongs fit tightly around the can. Allow the water to boil and fill the can with steam. Have a pan of cold water next to you. Move the can over the water. Quickly turn the can upside down and place it in the cold water. Be sure the opening to the can is completely under water. It will look like an invisible hand reached around the can and crushed it.

The Investigative Problem
Does air have weight? Does air exert pressure? What are balanced and unbalanced forces?

22

Gather These Things:
- ✔ Small plastic cup (4 to 8 ounce)
- ✔ Large index card
- ✔ Sheet of paper
- ✔ Plastic tub or bucket

For Optional Activity
- ✔ Sheet of newspaper
- ✔ Table
- ✔ Safety glasses
- ✔ A thin yardstick or thin wooden strip (unfinished)

Procedure and Observations

1) Place your hands on your ribs and take a deep breath. Observe. Exhale. What did you observe when you inhaled and exhaled? Record your observations and try to think of an explanation for what caused this.

2) Stuff a crumpled sheet of paper into the bottom of a dry plastic cup. (A half sheet of paper may be enough.) Invert the cup and push it to the bottom of the tub of water. Carefully remove the cup, making sure not to tilt it as you take it out of the water. Is the paper wet or dry?

3) Fill a small plastic cup with water. Put an index card over the mouth of the cup. Hold the card in place and invert the cup of water. Do this over the plastic tub in case it spills. Don't squeeze the cup! Does the index card remain over the cup of water?

4) Optional. Place the yardstick or wooden strip on the table, leaving less than half of it sticking off the end. Lay a sheet of newspaper over the yardstick with the crease on the yardstick. Smooth out the newspaper, making sure to get as much air out from under the paper as you can. Wear your safety glasses. Hit the end of the yardstick hanging over the table with your fist as fast and hard as you can. What happened to the yardstick?

23

OBJECTIVES

Activity 5 examines the weight and pressure of the air around us. Students recognize that air has weight, weight is a force, and air pressure is all around us. They observe that air pressure exerts a significant force, which often goes unnoticed because the forces are balanced. They recognize that mass and weight are different.

NOTE

The demonstration described in "Think About This" is dramatic and should be practiced before you do it for the class. It shows what happens when air pressure inside and outside of an object is unbalanced. It also illustrates how much air pressure there is around everything. Whenever you use a heat source, wear safety glasses and caution students to be a safe distance away. This is for your safety as well as to model safety to the students. An alcohol burner or a hot plate would provide enough heat to cause the water in the can to boil.

Put about 2 tablespoons of water in an empty aluminum soda can. Hold it with a pair of tongs and place it over a heat source. Be sure the tongs fit tightly around the can. Allow the water to boil and fill the can with steam. Have a pan of cold water next to you. Lift the can while it is still steaming in an upright position and move it over the water. Quickly turn the can upside-down and place it in the cold water. Be sure the opening to the can is completely under water. It will look like an invisible hand reached around the can and crushed it.

You may also prefer to demonstrate the activity that calls for breaking a wooden stick.

The Science Stuff

Most things on earth are surrounded by an equal amount of pressure and have the same amount of pressure inside as they do outside. We usually only notice these forces when they become unbalanced. The can in the demonstration filled with steam, and most of the air was pushed out. When the can was turned upside down and placed in the cold water, the steam turned back into water. This left a very small amount of air inside the can. The air pressure on the outside remained the same, but the air pressure inside was much less. The air pressure pushing on the outside of the can was greater than the air pressure inside the can pushing out. The forces were unbalanced, so the can crumpled and collapsed.

Compare the two cans. In the first can, the air pressure inside the can was equal to the air pressure outside the can. The forces canceled each other out, so these were balanced forces. In the second can, the air pressure inside the can was reduced, while the air pressure outside remained the same. The forces did not cancel each other out, so the forces were unbalanced. The greater force outside the can was not opposed by an equal force inside the can.

At sea level we are sitting under a layer of air more than 80 miles thick. The total weight of the air above you is primarily what causes the air pressure on your body. Even though we can't see this air and may not notice it, air exerts a force on everything on earth. Air has weight (mass) and it takes up space. It also exerts pressure in every direction.

Your chest expands because the number of air molecules in your lungs increases. The tiny air molecules are invisible but they still have weight (mass) and take up space.

When you pushed the cup containing a crumpled sheet of paper under water, the paper did not get wet. Water couldn't enter the cup, because the air inside the cup had already taken up the space.

Air pressure at sea level can change as it gets cooler or warmer and as it gets dryer or moister. These small changes can have major effects on the weather. At higher elevations, air pressure will become a little less, because the air becomes less dense.

At sea level, air pressure is about 14.7 pounds on every square inch of any object that is surrounded by air. That means there are nearly 15 pounds of air pressure pushing on every square inch of you!

The reason the card did not fall off when you inverted the cup of water was because the air pressure was greater than the weight of the water. Assume the water weighed one pound. (It was probably less than this.) The weight of the water was the total downward force on the card. The upward force was almost 15 pounds on every square inch on the card. This much pressure was more than enough to hold the card in place.

your lungs

Making Connections

Have you ever had the breath knocked out of you? It feels like there is a very heavy weight on your chest, because the air above you is pushing down harder than the air in your lungs is pushing back. Once you fill your lungs with air again, the air pressure outside and inside will be balanced again.

If you have ever ridden in an airplane or traveled in the mountains, you probably noticed that your ears seemed to feel

balanced forces on can | air is pushed out of the can by steam | unbalanced forces on can | water | crushed can

24

If you did the optional investigation, the thin strip of wood probably broke when you hit it with your fist. The sheet of newspaper lying over the ruler had about 9300 pounds of air pressure above it and below it.

When you moved the yardstick slowly, you were able to raise the newspaper without breaking the yardstick. However, when you hit the yardstick the molecules of air above the paper could not move out of the way fast enough. The tremendous weight (pressure) of the air above the newspaper caused the yardstick to break.

Air pressure is all around you.

stopped up. Swallowing or yawning may have helped them feel better. This is an example of how changes in air pressure can affect you. As you go higher, the air pressure around you becomes less. That causes the air pressure pushing on the inside of your eardrum to be greater than the air pressure pushing on the outside of your eardrum. In other words, the forces pushing on the eardrum are unbalanced. Yawning may let them become balanced again.

Dig Deeper

Sometimes helium-filled weather balloons get turned loose in the air and they go very high in the air. As the balloons get higher, the air pressure around them gets less. What will happen to the balloons as the pressure outside gets less? As the balloon rises, the temperature gets colder. Will the temperature of the balloon affect its size? Do you think they will get larger, smaller, or stay the same? What do you think would happen if a balloon were released on the moon where there is no air? Make drawings of what you predict would happen to the size of the balloons in these situations. Give reasons for your predictions.

Look on some boxes of cake mix and find one that has two recipes for baking the cake — one for cooking at sea level and one for cooking on a mountain. What is different about the air pressure at sea level and the air pressure on a mountaintop that would affect how a cake bakes best? Did you know that boiling water is hotter at sea level than on a mountaintop? You might have to increase the cooking time to prepare a pan of peas for dinner on a mountaintop. See if you can provide an explanation for this.

Do some research on space suits. What is the purpose of space suits? When do astronauts wear them? Why do they wear them?

Try to find a scientific explanation for how a vacuum cleaner works.

What Did You Learn?

1. Does air have weight?
2. Does air fill the space inside an "empty" cup?
3. What is the pressure of air on every square inch at sea level?
4. Why don't we notice the weight of air on our bodies?
5. Why did the paper in the cup that was pushed underwater remain dry?
6. Is air pressure greater at sea level or on a mountaintop?
7. What would happen to a helium-filled balloon if the air pressure inside the balloon stays the same, but

the air pressure outside becomes less? (Assume the temperature is the same.)
8. What causes discomfort to your ears if you are riding up and down mountain roads?
9. What is the difference in balanced and unbalanced forces?
10. Is air pressure the same everywhere in the earth's atmosphere?
11. You did an activity in which a cup of water was covered with an index card and turned upside down. Explain why air pressure on the card was greater than the weight of the water.

25

WHAT DID YOU LEARN?

1. Does air have weight? *Yes.*

2. Does air fill the space inside an "empty" cup? *Yes.*

3. What is the pressure of air on every square inch at sea level? *A little less than 15 pounds on every square inch.*

4. Why don't we notice the weight of air on our bodies? *Because we experience the same amount of air pressure above and below, inside and outside.*

5. Why did the paper in the cup that was pushed under water remain dry? *Water couldn't enter the cup because it was already filled with air.*

6. Is air pressure greater at sea level or on a mountaintop? *At sea level.*

7. What happens to a helium-filled balloon if the air pressure inside the balloon stays the same, but the air pressure outside becomes less? (Assume the temperature is the same.) *The balloon will get bigger and may even burst.*

8. What causes discomfort to your ears if you are riding up and down mountain roads? *The air pressure inside and outside of your eardrum is not balanced.*

9. What is the difference in balanced and unbalanced forces? *Two balanced forces cancel each other out. An unbalanced force is not canceled out by another force. If two opposing forces are not equal, they are said to be unbalanced forces.*

10. Is air pressure the same everywhere in the earth's atmosphere? *No.*

11. You did an activity in which a cup of water was covered with an index card and turned upside down. Explain why air pressure on the card was greater than the weight of the water. *The force on the card from the water was equal to the weight of the water. The force on the card from the air pressure was equal to almost 15 pounds on every square inch. The air pressure was much greater than the weight of the water.*

Floating Pencil Race
Gravity versus Air Resistance

Think about This There was a time when U.S. astronauts actually landed on the moon and explored it firsthand. Two astronauts did a demonstration on the moon that was filmed and shown on TV. One astronaut held a hammer in one hand and a feather in the other hand at the same height. He dropped them at the same time. The hammer and the feather fell at the same rate of speed and hit the ground at the same time. On earth, the feather would fall much slower than a hammer. Why do you think the feather fell like the hammer on the moon?

Astronaut Harrison "Jack" Schmitt covered with lunar dirt, Apollo 17

The Investigative Problem
What are some ways that a pencil can be made to fall at a slower speed?

26

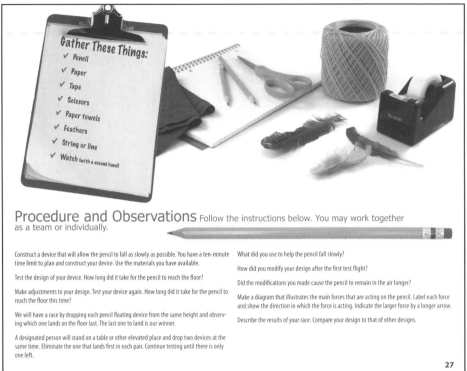

Gather These Things:
- ✔ Pencil
- ✔ Paper
- ✔ Tape
- ✔ Scissors
- ✔ Paper towels
- ✔ Feathers
- ✔ String or line
- ✔ Watch (with a second hand)

Procedure and Observations
Follow the instructions below. You may work together as a team or individually.

Construct a device that will allow the pencil to fall as slowly as possible. You have a ten-minute time limit to plan and construct your device. Use the materials you have available.

Test the design of your device. How long did it take for the pencil to reach the floor?

Make adjustments to your design. Test your device again. How long did it take for the pencil to reach the floor this time?

We will have a race by dropping each pencil floating device from the same height and observing which one lands on the floor last. The last one to land is our winner.

A designated person will stand on a table or other elevated place and drop two devices at the same time. Eliminate the one that lands first in each pair. Continue testing until there is only one left.

What did you use to help the pencil fall slowly?

How did you modify your design after the first test flight?

Did the modifications you made cause the pencil to remain in the air longer?

Make a diagram that illustrates the main forces that are acting on the pencil. Label each force and show the direction in which the force is acting. Indicate the larger force by a longer arrow.

Describe the results of your race. Compare your design to that of other designs.

27

OBJECTIVES Students recognize that weight (gravitational force) and air resistance and friction are forces. Weight (gravitational force) acts in the same direction the pencil is falling and air resistance/friction acts in an opposite direction to the pencil's movement. Air resistance is a kind of friction that opposes a falling object as it moves though the air. If the air resistance on the pencil is increased, the pencil will fall slower. Arrows are used to show direction and magnitude of the forces. Introduce the concepts of balanced and unbalanced forces. The forces acting on the falling pencil are unbalanced, because weight continues to be the larger force during falling.

NOTE Students should show that they understand the concept of opposing forces on a moving object by their use of arrows. When two forces are opposite, the arrows should show the directions of the forces, as well as the relative amounts of the forces. If one force is larger than another, the length of the arrow should indicate which is larger. Weight and gravitational force are very similar. For objects on the earth, weight is defined as the force of the earth's gravitational attraction for any object on or around the earth's surface.

The Science Stuff

A hammer and a feather fall at the same speed on the moon because there is no air around the moon. Thus, there is no air resistance on the feather as it falls. If astronauts tried to do today's activity on the moon, the parachute would not slow the pencil's fall.

There are upward and downward forces acting on the pencil as it falls. The pencil's weight (from the earth's gravity) is a force that pulls down on the pencil. There is some friction between the pencil and the air, which pushes up on the pencil. The upward force on the pencil can be greatly increased by connecting a parachute-like device to the pencil. The parachute produces more air resistance. In this activity, you are trying to make the air resistance greater, because you can't change the gravitational force on the pencil (the pencil's weight).

More than one force was acting on the pencil as it was falling. In this case, the weight of the pencil (gravitational force) was pulling down while the air resistance/friction was pushing up. The air resistance and friction forces partially canceled out the weight force. The overall force on the pencil was downward, but not as much as it would have been without the parachute.

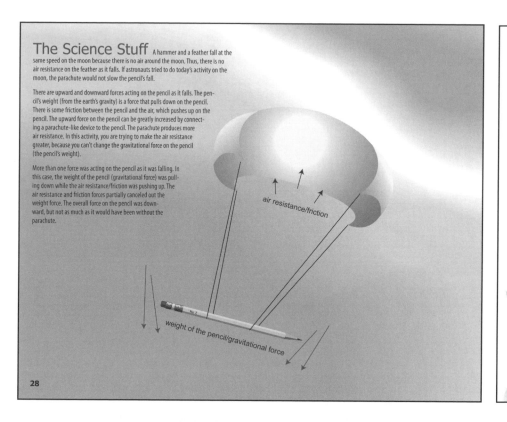

air resistance/friction

weight of the pencil/gravitational force

28

Making Connections

Think about how a parachute saves a person's life when a skydiver jumps out of an airplane and lands on the ground. The resistance of the air helps defy gravity, so the skydiver falls slowly and isn't injured when landing on the ground.

Even with a parachute, a skydiver falls through the air. However, there is a point where the diver stops accelerating and reaches "terminal velocity."

Dig Deeper
Find some more information about terminal velocity and how it applies to someone using a parachute.

Try making a parachute using different kinds of fabric. See if you can find some scraps of silk or some kind of thin fabric with a close weave, as well as another kind of fabric. Demonstrate your best and worst parachute to other students.

Do some research on the first parachutes. How were they made? How are modern parachutes different from the early models? Has skydiving become a sport today?

What Did You Learn?

1. What force pulled down on the pencil as it was falling?
2. What resulted in an upward push on the pencil as it was falling?
3. Why would this activity not slow the pencil if it were done on the moon?
4. In what direction does friction push on a moving object?
5. Is there gravity on the moon?
6. Is there air around the moon?
7. If an astronaut rubbed two rocks together on the moon, would there be friction between the rocks?

29

WHAT DID YOU LEARN?

1. What force pulled down on the pencil as it was falling? *Weight (gravitational force).*

2. What resulted in an upward push on the pencil as it was falling? *Air resistance/friction.*

3. Why would this activity not slow the pencil if it were done on the moon? *There is no air around the moon, so there would be no air resistance.*

4. In what direction does friction push on a moving object? *Opposite to the way in which the object is moving.*

5. Is there gravity on the moon? *Yes.*

6. Is there air around the moon? *No.*

7. If an astronaut rubbed two rocks together on the moon, would there be friction between the rocks? *Yes.*

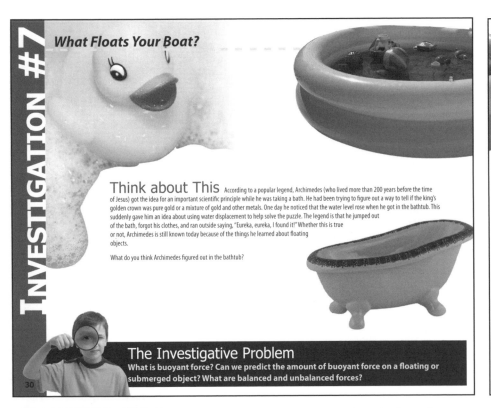

What Floats Your Boat?

Think about This
According to a popular legend, Archimedes (who lived more than 200 years before the time of Jesus) got the idea for an important scientific principle while he was taking a bath. He had been trying to figure out a way to tell if the king's golden crown was pure gold or a mixture of gold and other metals. One day he noticed that the water level rose when he got in the bathtub. This suddenly gave him an idea about using water displacement to help solve the puzzle. The legend is that he jumped out of the bath, forgot his clothes, and ran outside saying, "Eureka, eureka, I found it!" Whether this is true or not, Archimedes is still known today because of the things he learned about floating objects.

What do you think Archimedes figured out in the bathtub?

The Investigative Problem
What is buoyant force? Can we predict the amount of buoyant force on a floating or submerged object? What are balanced and unbalanced forces?

30

Gather These Things:
- ✓ Overflow cup (or a container with a spout)
- ✓ Empty film canister with lids
- ✓ 16 pennies (minted after 1982)
- ✓ Graduated cylinder
- ✓ Quart jar
- ✓ Water
- ✓ Liquid detergent
- ✓ Balance scales if available

! Remember to add the weight of the canister (5 grams) to the weight of the pennies each time and record under ... weight of cup + weight of pennies.

Procedure and Observations
Archimedes made an amazing discovery about the weight of the water that overflows when you put an object in it. He referred to the overflow as "displaced fluid." See if you can discover the same thing Archimedes did as you do this activity. Add two or three drops of liquid detergent to a quart of water. Get a container with a spout and fill it as full as you can with this water. Place a graduated cylinder beneath the spout.

Place eight pennies in the canister (cup #1). The canister weighs about 5 grams and each penny weighs about 2.5 grams, for a total of 25 grams. Predict whether cup #1 will sink or float. Record your prediction in the chart. Place cup #1 in the container with the spout and measure the amount of water that overflows in milliliters. Record this in the chart.

Add two more pennies to the canister and place the lid on it to keep all the water out. The empty canister weighs about 5 grams, and ten pennies weigh about 25 grams. This will be cup #2, and its total weight will be 30 grams. Predict whether or not the canister will sink or float. Refill the container with the spout and lower the canister into the container of water. Measure the water that is displaced. Repeat this process five times. Notice that the canister with eight pennies floats higher in the water than the canister with ten pennies. As you add more pennies, is there a point where the canister is almost underwater?

There is a neat trick you can do with a measured amount of water to determine its weight. One milliliter (mL) of water weighs exactly one gram (g). That means 10 mL of water weighs 10 g; 15 mL of water weighs 15 g, etc. Simply change the milliliters of overflowed water to grams and record in the last column. When you have finished the chart, look for number patterns.

Cup #	Weight of cup + weight of pennies	Prediction (float/ sink)	Observation (float/sink)	Milliliters of overflowed water	Weight of overflowed water in grams
1					
2					
3					
4					
5					

31

OBJECTIVES
Archimedes' principle is examined to show the force of buoyancy. Students use quantitative data to verify Archimedes' principle. They use examples to illustrate balanced and unbalanced forces. A floating boat illustrates balanced forces where weight (gravitational force) pulls down on the boat and buoyancy pushes up on the boat. The forces of weight and buoyancy will have a canceling effect on one another when the boat is floating. If the weight force becomes greater than the buoyant force, the forces on the boat will become unbalanced and the boat will sink.

If more than one force acts on an object along a straight line, then the forces will reinforce or cancel one another, depending on their direction and magnitude.

NOTE
This activity depends on being able to accurately measure the weight of the canisters and the volume of the displaced water. A graduated cylinder is used to measure the volume of the water. The surface of the water in a graduated cylinder will curve downward. When reading the volume of water in a cylinder, there will appear to be two levels of the water. Read the lower level. The upper line only contains a few drops of water that stick to the cylinder.

If you don't have graduated cylinders, you can fill medicine measures with water. A milliliter (mL) is the same amount as a cubic centimeter (cc or cm^3). Add the measured amount of water to a tall, skinny glass container with vertical sides. Place a strip of tape from the top to the bottom of the glass. Mark the milliliters of water on the tape. Repeat several times. If this sounds like too much trouble, you can simply order the equipment inexpensively.

Ideally, the students should have access to a good set of balance scales and know how to use them. If balance scales are available, take time to show the students how to use them and have them weigh the canister and the pennies each time. But if this is not an option, you can make some assumptions and still obtain accurate results. An empty film canister weighs about 5 grams. Pennies minted after 1982 weigh about 2.5 grams. (Older pennies weigh about 3 grams.)

Start with 8 new pennies, which will have a weight of 20 grams. The weight of the empty canister is about 5 grams, so the weight of canister #1 will be 25 grams. The weight of canister #2 will be the weight of an empty canister (5 grams) + 25 grams (weight of 10 pennies). Calculate the weight of cups 1 through 5 in this way.

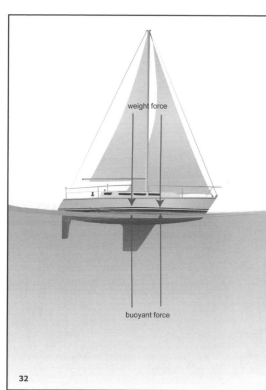

weight force

buoyant force

The Science Stuff
According to Archimedes' principle, if an object floats in water, its weight will equal the weight of the displaced water. Column two should equal column six for all the floating cups.

Even if a canister sinks, it is still buoyed up by a force equal to the weight of the displaced water. Have you ever tried to lift a heavy object that is underwater? The object feels much lighter underwater than it does out of the water, because the buoyant force of the water is pushing up on the object. It is much easier to lift a heavy object underwater than to lift the same object above the water.

The way Archimedes was able to tell if the king's crown was made of pure gold was to weigh the crown and then find its volume. He found the volume by putting the crown in a container of water and measuring the overflow. Next he obtained a block of pure gold. He weighed it and found its volume. Once he knew the weight (actually mass) and the volume of each, he could divide the volume by the weight and obtain the density of the crown. If the crown was made of pure gold, it would have the same density as the block of pure gold.

Large ships are made of heavy steel, although a bar of steel would quickly sink in water. The thing that determines whether or not the ship will float is the weight of the water it displaces. If the weight of the displaced water is equal to the weight of the ship, the ship will float. If the weight of the displaced water is less than the weight of the ship, the ship will sink. The upward force the water exerts on floating or sunken boats is called buoyant force.

Recall that when two forces oppose each other, they are said to be balanced when they cancel each other out. There are balanced forces acting on a floating ship. The weight of the ship (from the earth's gravitational force) pulls down. At the same time, the buoyant force on the ship pushes up. Therefore, the two forces cancel each other out, and the forces acting on the boat are balanced.

A force that is not completely canceled out by another force is said to be an unbalanced force. If the weight force becomes greater than the buoyant force, the forces acting on the ship will not be balanced and the ship will sink.

Making Connections
When cargo is added to a large boat, the boat floats deeper in the water. When the cargo is unloaded, the boat floats higher in the water.

Many people enjoy camping and canoeing trips. The total weight of the person in the canoe plus the equipment must be less than the weight of the water displaced by the boat. Heavier people may have to cut down on the supplies to keep their canoe afloat.

We observed that there are upward and downward forces acting on a floating boat. Forces do not necessarily cause objects to move. Consider a book lying on a table. You know that the weight of the book is a force that pushes down. But did you know that the support forces of the table push up? The upward and downward forces on the book are balanced. However, if the weight of the book were greater than the table's support forces, the forces would be unbalanced and the book would break through the table and fall down.

Dig Deeper
Take two equal amounts of aluminum foil and design an object that will sink and an object that will float in a container of water. Use Archimedes' principle to explain why the two objects have the same weight, but one will float and one will sink in water.

See if you can discover the difference in an object floating in pure water and that same object floating in salt water by doing an experiment. What did you find out?

The dimensions of Noah's ark are given in Genesis in units called cubits. Convert cubits to a more familiar unit. Compare the size and shape of the ark to some modern-day ships.

Santa Maria   Wyoming   Titanic   Queen Mary 6
WOOD SHIPS   STEEL SHIPS
Noah's Ark

What Did You Learn?
1. Archimedes used a method known as water displacement to measure what?
2. If you know the volume and the weight (mass) of an object, you can calculate what?
3. Archimedes discovered that there is a buoyant force on objects in water (and all fluids) that is equal to what?
4. Water also exerts a buoyant force on objects that sink in water (or in fluids) that is equal to what?
5. Make a drawing of a boat that is floating in water and label the main upward and downward forces acting on the boat.
6. Which would displace the most water — a solid block of iron or a boat made from the same block of iron?
7. How can you make a piece of aluminum sink and also make an equal piece of aluminum float?
8. Look up Archimedes' principle in a reference book or online and rewrite this principle in your own words. Instead of water, what word does Archimedes use?
9. Why does a heavy object feel lighter under water than it does out of water?
10. Does the upward buoyant force on a floating boat cancel out the downward force of weight?
11. If the weight of a floating boat becomes greater than the buoyant force on the boat, are the forces on the boat balanced or unbalanced?

32

33

WHAT DID YOU LEARN?

1. **Archimedes used a method known as water displacement to measure what?** *The volume of an irregular solid and the volume of the water a floating object displaces.*

2. **If you know the volume and the weight of an object, you can calculate what?** *The density of the object.*

3. **Archimedes discovered that there is a buoyant force on objects in water (and all fluids) that is equal to what?** *The weight of the displaced water.*

4. **Water also exerts a buoyant force on objects that sink in water (or in fluids) that is equal to what?** *The weight of the displaced water.*

5. **Make a drawing of a boat that is floating in water and label the main upward force and downward force acting on the boat.**

6. **Which would displace the most water — a solid block of iron or a boat made from the same block of iron?** *A boat made from a block of iron, because it would displace more water than a solid block of iron of equal weight.*

7. **How can you make a piece of aluminum sink and also make an equal piece of aluminum float?** *A piece of aluminum pressed into a tight ball will sink, but an equal piece of aluminum made into the shape of a boat will float.*

8. **Look up Archimedes' principle in a reference book or online and rewrite this principle in your own words. Instead of water, what word does Archimedes use?** *Archimedes uses the word "fluid" instead of water, because fluid includes both liquids and gases. His principle says that there is an upward force on floating objects that is equal to the weight of the fluid the object displaces. This same force pushes up on an object that sinks in a fluid.*

9. **Why does a heavy object feel lighter underwater than it does out of water?** *When an object is underwater, it is being pushed up by a buoyant force that is equal to the weight of the water the object displaces. This buoyant force helps you to lift the object as long as it is underwater.*

10. **Does the upward buoyant force on a floating boat cancel out the downward force of weight?** *Yes.*

11. **If the weight of a floating boat becomes greater than the buoyant force on the boat, are the forces on the boat balanced or unbalanced?** *Unbalanced.*

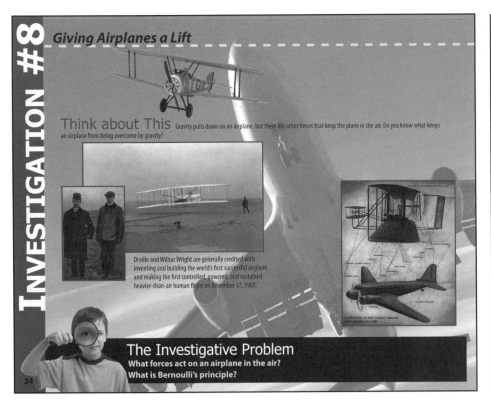

INVESTIGATION #8

Giving Airplanes a Lift

Think about This Gravity pulls down on an airplane, but there are other forces that keep the plane in the air. Do you know what keeps an airplane from being overcome by gravity?

Orville and Wilbur Wright are generally credited with inventing and building the world's first successful airplane and making the first controlled, powered, and sustained heavier-than-air human flight on December 17, 1903.

The Investigative Problem
What forces act on an airplane in the air?
What is Bernoulli's principle?

34

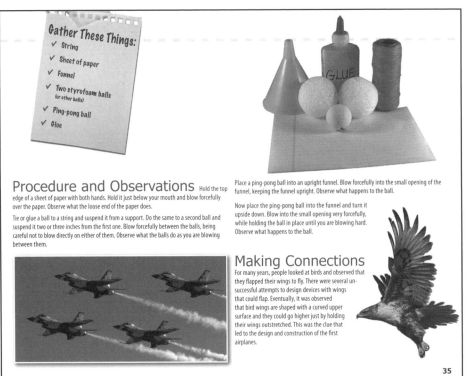

Gather These Things:
- ✓ String
- ✓ Sheet of paper
- ✓ Funnel
- ✓ Two styrofoam balls (or other balls)
- ✓ Ping-pong ball
- ✓ Glue

Procedure and Observations
Hold the top edge of a sheet of paper with both hands. Hold it just below your mouth and blow forcefully over the paper. Observe what the loose end of the paper does.

Tie or glue a ball to a string and suspend it from a support. Do the same to a second ball and suspend it two or three inches from the first one. Blow forcefully between the balls, being careful not to blow directly on either of them. Observe what the balls do as you are blowing between them.

Place a ping-pong ball into an upright funnel. Blow forcefully into the small opening of the funnel, keeping the funnel upright. Observe what happens to the ball.

Now place the ping-pong ball into the funnel and turn it upside down. Blow into the small opening very forcefully, while holding the ball in place until you are blowing hard. Observe what happens to the ball.

Making Connections
For many years, people looked at birds and observed that they flapped their wings to fly. There were several unsuccessful attempts to design devices with wings that could flap. Eventually, it was observed that bird wings are shaped with a curved upper surface and they could go higher just by holding their wings outstretched. This was the clue that led to the design and construction of the first airplanes.

35

OBJECTIVES Bernoulli's principle is examined to illustrate how airplanes achieve lift. As students experience examples of Bernoulli's principle, they should be able to express this principle in their own words. Students should recognize that when an airplane is in flight, the upward force of lift is balanced by the downward force of the airplane's weight.

NOTE A strong wind will exert a strong pressure straight ahead. It is the sideways (internal) pressure that is reduced. The faster the wind moves, the less the internal pressure becomes. The activities will illustrate this principle even though it may not "sound right" to students at first. Take time to discuss each activity and compare what students observe to the diagrams.

WHAT DID YOU LEARN?

1. What is the name of the force that pushes upward on an airplane wing? *Lift.*

2. What is the force that pulls downward on an airplane wing? *Weight of the airplane (the earth's gravitational attraction on the plane).*

3. What is there about the shape of an airplane wing that causes the air pressure to be greater under the wing than it is over the wing? *The air pressure inside a column of air is less where the air is moving faster. Wings have a curved shape on top while the bottom of the wing is flat. The air has to move faster over the top of the wing than it does under the wing.*

4. Make a drawing of the two balls you blew between. Use arrows to show which is greater — the air pressure in the moving column of air or the normal air pressure outside the balls. *Drawing of balls, showing greater air pressure outside the balls than between them.*

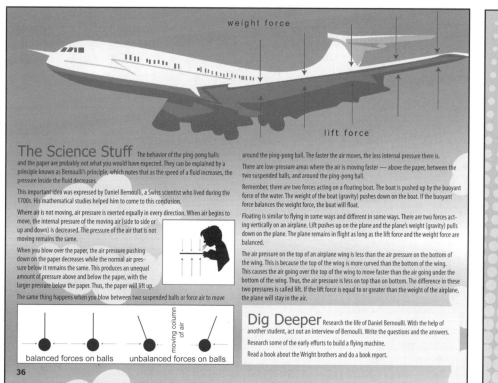

weight force

lift force

The Science Stuff

The behavior of the ping-pong balls and the paper are probably not what you would have expected. They can be explained by a principle known as Bernoulli's principle, which notes that as the speed of a fluid increases, the pressure inside the fluid decreases.

This important idea was expressed by Daniel Bernoulli, a Swiss scientist who lived during the 1700s. His mathematical studies helped him to come to this conclusion.

Where air is not moving, air pressure is exerted equally in every direction. When air begins to move, the internal pressure of the moving air (side to side or up and down) is decreased. The pressure of the air that is not moving remains the same.

When you blow over the paper, the air pressure pushing down on the paper decreases while the normal air pressure below it remains the same. This produces an unequal amount of pressure above and below the paper, with the larger pressure below the paper. Thus, the paper will lift up.

The same thing happens when you blow between two suspended balls or force air to move

around the ping-pong ball. The faster the air moves, the less internal pressure there is.

There are low-pressure areas where the air is moving faster — above the paper, between the two suspended balls, and around the ping-pong ball.

Remember, there are two forces acting on a floating boat. The boat is pushed up by the buoyant force of the water. The weight of the boat (gravity) pushes down on the boat. If the buoyant force balances the weight force, the boat will float.

Floating is similar to flying in some ways and different in some ways. There are two forces acting vertically on an airplane. Lift pushes up on the plane and the plane's weight (gravity) pulls down on the plane. The plane remains in flight as long as the lift force and the weight force are balanced.

The air pressure on the top of an airplane wing is less than the air pressure on the bottom of the wing. This is because the top of the wing is more curved than the bottom of the wing. This causes the air going over the top of the wing to move faster than the air going under the bottom of the wing. Thus, the air pressure is less on top than on bottom. The difference in these two pressures is called lift. If the lift force is equal to or greater than the weight of the airplane, the plane will stay in the air.

Dig Deeper

Research the life of Daniel Bernoulli. With the help of another student, act out an interview of Bernoulli. Write the questions and the answers.

Research some of the early efforts to build a flying machine.

Read a book about the Wright brothers and do a book report.

balanced forces on balls   unbalanced forces on balls   moving column of air

36

What Did You Learn?

1. What is the name of the force that pushes upward on an airplane wing?
2. What is the force that pulls downward on an airplane wing?
3. What is there about the shape of an airplane wing that causes the air pressure to be greater under the wing than it is over the wing?
4. Make a drawing of the two balls you blew between. Use arrows to show which is greater — the air pressure in the moving column of air or the normal air pressure outside the balls.
5. Make a drawing of the paper you blew over. Use arrows to show the pressure on top of the paper and the pressure under the paper.
6. What is the definition of lift?
7. State Bernoulli's principle in your own words.
8. What two forces on an airplane must be opposite and equal for the airplane to maintain its altitude?

It's My Tree, I Built a Nest in It

Dyan's favorite place was the big oak tree that stood next to his uncle's house. Dyan dreamed often of the great tree that shaded everyone from the hot sun.

One day his uncle said, "Dyan, I have a gift for you. There is an acorn in this box to take home with you. Find a place near the edge of your father's garden, dig a large hole, and fill it with the best soil around. Then plant the little acorn there and water it every day until it sprouts."

Dyan thanked his uncle many times. He did everything exactly as his uncle had told him to do, and before long a tiny oak tree began to grow.

Dyan wished it would grow faster, but it made him happy to dream about the day when it would become a big tree. As Dyan grew taller, so did the tree. One summer he noticed the tree had grown taller than his father.

Then the time came when Dyan was a man. He built a new house close to the oak tree for himself and his wife. New branches grew each year and old branches became stronger. Dyan's family also grew as a son was added to his family.

It wasn't long before there were black birds sitting in the tree. They were called geezy birds by the people in the local village. The birds soon built nests in the oak tree. They squawked loudly and threateningly at all the animals and

the other birds who ventured too close. They argued and fought day and night over who had the right to each square inch of the tree.

Dyan and his wife were too busy farming and taking care of their young family to do much about the geezy birds. Dyan didn't like the irritating noises they made or the smelly mess they made under the tree, and he knew he would have to get rid of them sometime.

Then one day, his young son went outside to play under the tree, and the meanest birds swooped down, pecking and clawing the little boy until he ran inside, crying and frightened.

Dyan was furious as he saw his son scratched and bleeding from the bird attack. He asked his son, "Who owns this tree — us or the birds? The birds think they do, because they built their nests and perch in the branches. But this is my tree that I planted and nourished so that my children could play in its shade. The birds will have to go."

With that, he proceeded to chase away the birds. He destroyed their nests and cleaned up the mess the birds had made underneath the tree. When he finished, it was just as he had dreamed it would be — a beautiful and safe place for his children and his family to enjoy.

The question is, who owned the oak tree — the birds that built nests and perched in its branches or the man who planted the acorn seed in his field?

The bigger question is who owns the earth — the people who live on earth and build their homes here or the One who planned and created the people and the earth?

How you answer this question is very important, because it becomes one of the foundations of your world view — how you think about everything. If you recognize that God created the heavens and the earth, then you will also understand that He is the owner and He makes the rules. Knowing that we are ultimately accountable to Him, we will live our lives with that in mind.

If you think there is no God, that He is not important, or that He has no interest in what you do, then you will think and act very differently about everything. You will likely make up your own rules about how to live, and you will not be too concerned about how God wants you to live.

God created all the matter and energy that exists in the universe. He also created the laws and principles by which all of nature operates. He expects us to acknowledge His lordship over all of His creation.

Read Psalm 24:1, Psalm 50:10–11, Psalm 89:11, Haggai 2:8, and Job 41:11. What do all of these verses tell us about God?

Why is it important to understand this?

37

It's My Tree, I Built a Nest In It

5. Make a drawing of the paper you blew over. Use arrows to show the pressure on top of the paper and the pressure under the paper.

6. What is the definition of lift? *Upward force on a wing or an airplane.*

7. State Bernoulli's principle in your own words. *Whenever a liquid or gas speeds up, its internal pressure becomes less.*

8. What two forces on an airplane must be opposite and equal for the airplane to maintain its altitude? *Weight and lift.*

Note: This is a good opportunity to talk about world views — what they are and why they are important. Our world views are formed according to how we choose to answer a few basic questions, such as: Who am I? Where did I come from? Why am I here? How do I live? Where I am going? If we recognize that God planned, designed, and created us according to His purposes, then we will have a basis for all of the basic questions of life. We will understand that He is the owner of everything, and He has the right to make the rules. Knowing that we are ultimately accountable to Him, we will live our lives with that in mind.

If someone thinks there is no God, that He is not important, or that He has no interest in what you do, that person will develop a very different world view.

Psalm 24:1, Psalm 50:10–11, Psalm 89:11, Haggai 2:8, and Job 41 tell us that God is the maker and owner of the earth. This is important to understand for many reasons. One reason is that this inevitably becomes a foundational part of our world view.

INVESTIGATION #9

Crash Test Dummies
Inertia and That Sudden Stop

Think about This Juan was in the highest gear on his bike as he tried to make the curve, but a little loose gravel caused him to lose his balance and tip over. He hit the ground at 15 miles per hour. Unfortunately, his body continued to travel straight ahead at 15 miles per hour until friction took over and finally stopped his movement. Knee pads, elbow pads, and a helmet minimized the damage. Juan just learned about inertia and Newton's first law of motion the hard way.

The Investigative Problem
Why is it hard to get things to start moving? Why is it hard to get moving things to stop?

Gather These Things:
- ✓ Skateboard
- ✓ 3 x 5 card
- ✓ Doll
- ✓ Long sheet of paper
- ✓ Plastic cup
- ✓ Small wooden blocks
- ✓ Toy car that rolls
- ✓ Board for ramp
- ✓ Small ruler
- ✓ Ball
- ✓ Penny
- ✓ Tape

Procedure and Observations

Part A.

Push the skateboard with your hand. Continue to hold the skateboard with your hand to keep it moving. What keeps it moving?

Push the skateboard and let go. Does it keep on moving?

Place the ball in the center of the board and give the board a push from the back. Be sure the block is taped to the back of the board. What happens to the ball?

Now place the ball at the back of the board and push the board toward the wall. What happens?

Put the doll on the back of the board and push the board toward the wall. What happens?

Discuss what happens in Part A before doing Part B.

Part B.

Try these activities. Tell what happens and give an explanation for what happens in terms of Newton's first law of motion.

(1) Put a penny on a card. Put the card over the opening of a plastic cup. Flick the card with your finger.

(2) Place a long piece of paper near the edge of a table and let about half the paper hang over the table. Stack some blocks on the paper. Hold the paper up with one hand and hit the paper quickly with a ruler.

(3) Place a penny on the top of a toy car. Let the car roll down a ramp that has a barrier at the end of the ramp.

Making Connections

Have you ever been standing in a bus or a train when it starts moving? Your body's inertia tends to keep you in the same place, but the place where you were standing moved away, dragging you with it.

OBJECTIVES

The concept of inertia is reinforced. Students see that once an object is in motion, it tends to keep on moving in a straight line and at the same speed, even though it is on or in an object that stops. They also observe that once an object is at rest, it tends to remain at rest. Objects start to move when an unbalanced force acts on it. An object stops moving when an unbalanced force acts on it.

NOTE

It is suggested that everyone do Part A first. They should discuss what happened and try to explain the results by using Newton's first law of motion. You could either demonstrate the Part B activities or have the students do them. They are all illustrations of Newton's first law of motion. Students should be able to give simple explanations for what happens.

The Science Stuff

Part A.

When you pushed the skateboard with your hand, the force of your hand kept it in motion. When you pushed the skateboard and let go, the skateboard's inertia kept it in motion.

Why did the ball move to the back of the board? The skateboard moved forward when you pushed on the back. There was no force put on the ball. It may have seemed that the ball rolled to the back of the board, but actually the back of the board came forward and met the ball while the ball remained in place. Once the block on the back of the board came in contact with the ball, it exerted a force on the ball and then the ball moved.

Why did the ball continue to move toward the wall even though the skateboard stopped? When the skateboard hit the wall, it stopped because the wall acted on the skateboard and caused it to stop. When the board stopped, the ball continued moving until it also hit the wall. This is the same reason the doll hit the wall, and why you should always wear your seat belt.

Part B.

(1) When you flicked the card with your finger, you exerted a force on the card, but not on the penny. The penny was not in motion, and the friction between the card and the penny was too small to cause the penny to move. The penny remained at rest until gravity pulled it down.

(2) When you hit the paper quickly with a ruler, the paper moved, but the blocks remained where they were stacked. A force moved the paper, but not the blocks. The friction between the paper and the blocks was very small. The blocks remained at rest throughout this activity, because they were not acted upon by an unbalanced force.

(3) A barrier stopped the car that was traveling down the ramp, but the penny on the car continued to travel straight ahead. A force stopped the car, but the penny was in motion and it continued to move forward at the same speed. Eventually the unbalanced forces of gravity and friction caused it to stop.

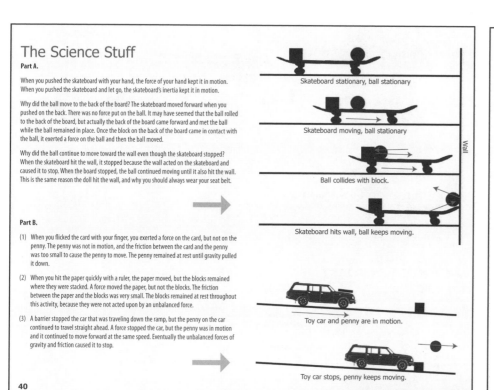

Skateboard stationary, ball stationary

Skateboard moving, ball stationary

Ball collides with block.

Skateboard hits wall, ball keeps moving.

Toy car and penny are in motion.

Toy car stops, penny keeps moving.

40

Wall

Dig Deeper
Try to find at least five other examples of how an object's inertia affects its ability to stop or start (such as the newton cradle pendulums below). You may include hypothetical (but realistic) examples of how things would move in space.

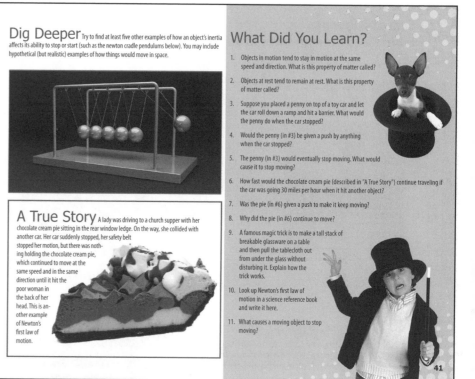

A True Story
A lady was driving to a church supper with her chocolate cream pie sitting in the rear window ledge. On the way, she collided with another car. Her car suddenly stopped, her safety belt stopped her motion, but there was nothing holding the chocolate cream pie, which continued to move at the same speed and in the same direction until it hit the poor woman in the back of her head. This is another example of Newton's first law of motion.

What Did You Learn?

1. Objects in motion tend to stay in motion at the same speed and direction. What is this property of matter called?

2. Objects at rest tend to remain at rest. What is this property of matter called?

3. Suppose you placed a penny on top of a toy car and let the car roll down a ramp and hit a barrier. What would the penny do when the car stopped?

4. Would the penny (in #3) be given a push by anything when the car stopped?

5. The penny (in #3) would eventually stop moving. What would cause it to stop moving?

6. How fast would the chocolate cream pie (described in "A True Story") continue traveling if the car was going 30 miles per hour when it hit another object?

7. Was the pie (in #6) given a push to make it keep moving?

8. Why did the pie (in #6) continue to move?

9. A famous magic trick is to make a tall stack of breakable glassware on a table and then pull the tablecloth out from under the glass without disturbing it. Explain how the trick works.

10. Look up Newton's first law of motion in a science reference book and write it here.

11. What causes a moving object to stop moving?

41

WHAT DID YOU LEARN?

1. Objects in motion tend to stay in motion at the same speed and direction. What is this property of matter called? *Inertia.*

2. Objects at rest tend to remain at rest. What is this property of matter called? *Inertia.*

3. Suppose you placed a penny on top of a toy car and let the car roll down a ramp and hit a barrier. What would the penny do when the car stopped? *The penny would move straight ahead at the same speed until friction and gravity acted on it.*

4. Would the penny (in #3) be given a push by anything when the car stopped? *No, it would simply keep moving in the same way it was already moving.*

5. The penny (in #3) would eventually stop moving. What would cause it to stop moving? *Forces of friction and the earth's gravitational pull.*

6. How fast would the chocolate cream pie (described in "A True Story") continue traveling if the car were going 30 miles per hour when it hit another object? *It would continue traveling at 30 miles per hour until unbalanced forces acted on it.*

7. Was the pie (in #6) given a push to make it keep moving? *No.*

8. Why did the pie (in #6) continue to move? *Objects in motion continue to move in the same direction unless an unbalanced force acts on it. This is a property of all matter.*

9. A famous magician trick is to make a tall stack of breakable glassware on a table and then pull the tablecloth out from under the glass without disturbing it. Explain how the trick works. *The tablecloth is always made of a smooth fabric with no hem or rough places in it. A force is applied to the tablecloth, which makes it move. The glassware's inertia causes it to remain at rest, because the force of the tablecloth moving under it is so slight.*

10. Look up Newton's first law of motion in a science reference book and write it here. *If an object is not moving, it will not start to move unless an unbalanced force is applied to it. If an object is moving, it will continue to move at the same speed in a straight line unless an unbalanced force is applied to it.*

11. What causes a moving object to stop moving? *Some kind of unbalanced force.*

INVESTIGATION #10

Cars and Ramps
What Does Newton Have to Say?

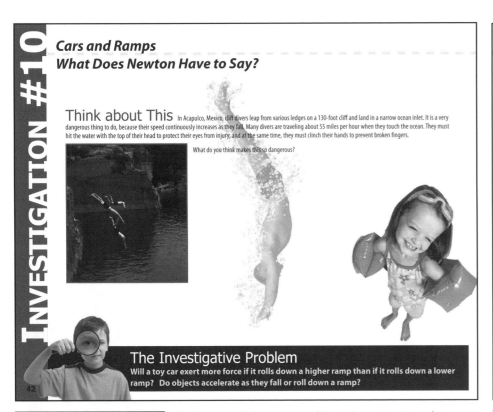

Think about This
In Acapulco, Mexico, cliff divers leap from various ledges on a 130-foot cliff and land in a narrow ocean inlet. It is a very dangerous thing to do, because their speed continuously increases as they fall. Many divers are traveling about 55 miles per hour when they touch the ocean. They must hit the water with the top of their head to protect their eyes from injury, and at the same time, they must clinch their hands to prevent broken fingers.

What do you think makes this so dangerous?

The Investigative Problem
Will a toy car exert more force if it rolls down a higher ramp than if it rolls down a lower ramp? Do objects accelerate as they fall or roll down a ramp?

42

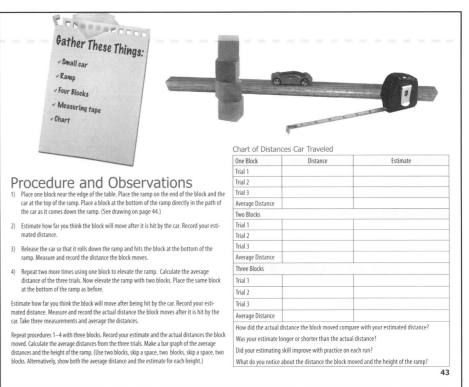

Gather These Things:
- ✓ Small car
- ✓ Ramp
- ✓ Four Blocks
- ✓ Measuring tape
- ✓ Chart

Procedure and Observations

1) Place one block near the edge of the table. Place the ramp on the end of the block and the car at the top of the ramp. Place a block at the bottom of the ramp directly in the path of the car as it comes down the ramp. (See drawing on page 44.)

2) Estimate how far you think the block will move after it is hit by the car. Record your estimated distance.

3) Release the car so that it rolls down the ramp and hits the block at the bottom of the ramp. Measure and record the distance the block moves.

4) Repeat two more times using one block to elevate the ramp. Calculate the average distance of the three trials. Now elevate the ramp with two blocks. Place the same block at the bottom of the ramp as before.

Estimate how far you think the block will move after being hit by the car. Record your estimated distance. Measure and record the actual distance the block moves after it is hit by the car. Take three measurements and average the distances.

Repeat procedures 1–4 with three blocks. Record your estimate and the actual distances the block moved. Calculate the average distances from the three trials. Make a bar graph of the average distances and the height of the ramp. (Use two blocks, skip a space, two blocks, skip a space, two blocks. Alternatively, show both the average distance and the estimate for each height.)

Chart of Distances Car Traveled

One Block	Distance	Estimate
Trial 1		
Trial 2		
Trial 3		
Average Distance		
Two Blocks		
Trial 1		
Trial 2		
Trial 3		
Average Distance		
Three Blocks		
Trial 1		
Trial 2		
Trial 3		
Average Distance		

How did the actual distance the block moved compare with your estimated distance?
Was your estimate longer or shorter than the actual distance?
Did your estimating skill improve with practice on each run?
What do you notice about the distance the block moved and the height of the ramp?

43

OBJECTIVES

Students recall that once an object is in motion, it tends to keep on moving in a straight line and at the same speed even though it is on or in another object that stops. A continuously applied unbalanced force (weight or gravity) will accelerate an object. Students are reminded that friction and gravity are both forces, and they act on the cars in opposite ways. The unbalanced force of gravity (weight) maintains a constant pull on the cars, even though it is offset a little by the opposing force of friction. Unbalanced forces will cause changes in the speed or direction of an object's motion.

NOTE

The emphasis in this lesson is on forces and acceleration. Acceleration can refer to going faster and faster or to going slower and slower. A similar activity is presented in the Energy book, where the emphasis is on energy. Newton's second law is usually found written as a mathematical formula. The concept that greater acceleration produces more force will probably be worth more than trying to understand the formula. Coming down the ramp, the cars will go faster and faster. After hitting the block, the cars will go slower and slower. Let the activities lead to the formation of this concept.

The Science Stuff

Do you remember that all matter has a tendency to keep moving once it starts moving? For example, if a toy car were pushed across a smooth table, it would keep moving straight ahead at the same speed until friction caused it to slow down and stop.

When the toy car was released from the top of the ramp, it was continuously pulled down by an unbalanced force. In this case, the unbalanced force is caused by the earth's gravitational pull on the car. The pull of gravity on the car is also its weight.

Therefore, instead of continuing to move at the same speed, the toy car kept going faster and faster. This constant change in speed is known as acceleration. Acceleration happens when objects are continually pushed or pulled by an unbalanced force.

The cars that are released from the highest points will accelerate the most as they reach the bottom of the ramp. The cars that accelerate the most will also exert the most force on the block. The more force the cars have, the farther the block will move.

These principles were studied by Isaac Newton and are written as Newton's second law of motion. This law shows how force, mass (weight), and acceleration are related. Think of acceleration as going faster and faster or as going slower and slower.

Newton's second law helps explain why cliff diving is so dangerous. The divers are constantly going faster and faster as they fall through the air and may reach speeds greater than 50 miles per hour. They have to reverse this accelerating process in order to stop. If they hit a hard surface at this speed, they would suddenly go from 50 miles per hour to 0 miles per hour in less than a second. This would cause the force of impact to be huge. However, if they enter the water smoothly and let their bodies slow down gradually while under the water, the force of impact is not too great.

There are at least two forces acting on the cars as they move. The weight of the cars is a downward force. Friction is a force that is pushing back on them. These two forces are not balanced, because the weight force (gravitational force) is larger than the force of friction.

The more height an object has, the more potential energy it has, and the more speed it will gain. This is true of the cars that started from the highest points, as well as the divers that jumped from the highest points. Keep this idea in mind. Stopping quickly results in a big impact force, and stopping gradually results in a small impact force.

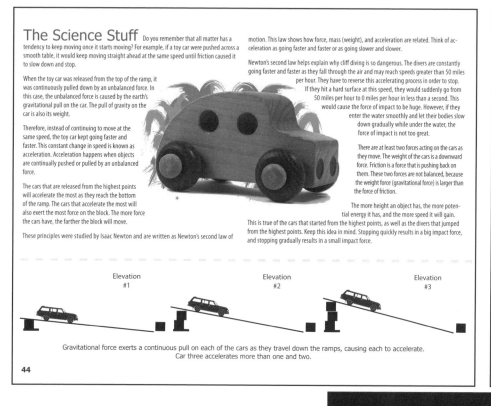

Elevation #1

Elevation #2

Elevation #3

Gravitational force exerts a continuous pull on each of the cars as they travel down the ramps, causing each to accelerate. Car three accelerates more than one and two.

44

Dig Deeper

Roller coasters are rides found at many amusement parks. The carts are pulled up to the starting point by an engine. However, once they start moving, the engine no longer pushes them. Do some reading about roller coasters to find how the rides are exciting, but safe. Remember, going down the hills, the riders go faster and faster. Going up the hills, the riders go slower and slower.

Making Connections

There is gravity in space, but a condition known as weightlessness occurs when an object's weight is balanced by the falling speed of the space vehicle. If you tried to do this experiment in a weightless state, the cars would not move unless they were pushed by an unbalanced force. Even if they were pushed, they would not roll down a ramp. Rather, they would move straight ahead at the same speed unless some kind of force caused them to stop, slow down, or change direction.

What Did You Learn?

1. Why would a car travel farther coming off a higher ramp than it would coming off a lower ramp?

2. Why would a car coming off a higher ramp push a block farther than a car coming off a lower ramp?

3. If you slide down a snow-covered hill on a sled, will your speed remain the same all the way down or will you travel faster and faster until you reach the bottom?

4. One thing that is explained by Newton's second law of motion is that the faster a falling object comes to a stop, the _____ its impact force will be.

5. What force caused the cars to move down the ramp?

6. Once the cars began to move, what caused them to stop moving?

7. Define acceleration in your own words.

8. Compare the speed at which the Mexico cliff divers are traveling when they hit the water to the speed you would be traveling from a high diving board at a swimming pool — much slower, about the same, or much faster.

45

WHAT DID YOU LEARN?

1. **Why would a car travel farther coming off a higher ramp than it would coming off a lower ramp?** *A continuously applied unbalanced force will cause changes in the car's speed. (It will also have more potential energy on the higher ramp.)*

2. **Why would a car coming off a higher ramp push a block farther than a car coming off a lower ramp?** *The faster the car is traveling, the greater the impact force will be.*

3. **If you slide down a snow-covered hill on a sled, will your speed remain the same all the way down or will you travel faster and faster until you reach the bottom?** *You will travel faster and faster until you reach the bottom.*

4. **One thing that is explained by Newton's second law of motion is that the faster a falling object comes to a stop, the _____ its impact force will be.** *Greater.*

5. **What force caused the cars to move down the ramp?** *The car was pulled down by an unbalanced force — the weight of the car or the earth's gravitational pull.*

6. **Once the cars began to move, what caused them to stop moving?** *The unbalanced forces of friction and the moving barrier caused them to stop moving.*

7. **Define acceleration in your own words.** *Acceleration is when an object keeps on changing its speed by going faster and faster or by going slower and slower. (Technically, it can also be when an object keeps on changing its direction, but most students probably won't understand this part of the definition.)*

8. **Compare the speed at which the Mexico cliff divers are traveling when they hit the water to the speed you would be traveling from a high diving board at a swimming pool — much slower, about the same, or much faster.** *The Mexico cliff divers will be traveling much faster than a swimming pool diver when they hit the water.*

The Mighty Conquering Catapults

Think about This For many years, spears, swords, and bow and arrows were the chief weapons of war. Then about 340 B.C., the Greeks invented the catapults. These devices could launch heavy missiles much farther than even the most powerful bows could shoot their arrows. By 200 B.C. the Romans had refined the invention. They were able to use catapults to launch heavy rocks that weighed 60 or more pounds as far as the length of five football fields. City walls were at one time an important defense for the people inside. However, catapults could damage the walls or hurl huge rocks over the walls.

The Investigative Problem

How does a catapult work?
What does a catapult have to do with Newton's first and second laws of motion?

46

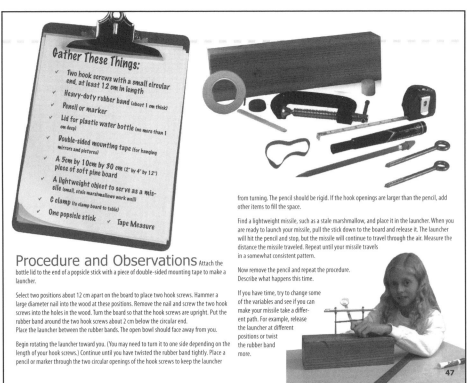

Gather These Things:

- ✓ Two hook screws with a small circular end, at least 12 cm in length
- ✓ Heavy-duty rubber band (about 1 cm thick)
- ✓ Pencil or marker
- ✓ Lid for plastic water bottle (no more than 1 cm deep)
- ✓ Double-sided mounting tape (for hanging mirrors and pictures)
- ✓ A 5cm by 10cm by 30 cm (2" by 4" by 12") piece of soft pine board
- ✓ A lightweight object to serve as a missile (small, stale marshmallows work well)
- ✓ C clamp (to clamp board to table)
- ✓ One popsicle stick   ✓ Tape Measure

Procedure and Observations
Attach the bottle lid to the end of a popsicle stick with a piece of double-sided mounting tape to make a launcher.

Select two positions about 12 cm apart on the board to place two hook screws. Hammer a large diameter nail into the wood at these positions. Remove the nail and screw the two hook screws into the holes in the wood. Turn the board so that the hook screws are upright. Put the rubber band around the two hook screws about 2 cm below the circular end. Place the launcher between the rubber bands. The open bowl should face away from you.

Begin rotating the launcher toward you. (You may need to turn it to one side depending on the length of your hook screws.) Continue until you have twisted the rubber band tightly. Place a pencil or marker through the two circular openings of the hook screws to keep the launcher

from turning. The pencil should be rigid. If the hook openings are larger than the pencil, add other items to fill the space.

Find a lightweight missile, such as a stale marshmallow, and place it in the launcher. When you are ready to launch your missile, pull the stick down to the board and release it. The launcher will hit the pencil and stop, but the missile will continue to travel through the air. Measure the distance the missile traveled. Repeat until your missile travels in a somewhat consistent pattern.

Now remove the pencil and repeat the procedure. Describe what happens this time.

If you have time, try to change some of the variables and see if you can make your missile take a different path. For example, release the launcher at different positions or twist the rubber band more.

47

OBJECTIVES Students again observe that once a missile is put into motion, it will tend to keep moving at the same speed and in the same direction until gravity and friction slow and stop its motion. The catapult launcher is continually pulled by an unbalanced force, causing it to go faster and faster (accelerate). The greater the acceleration, the greater the force there will be.

NOTE The wooden board and the two hook screws can be saved for activity #19. It may be necessary to use a pair of pliers to bend the end of the screw into a circular opening. As a caution, be sure the students use a lightweight object, such as a paper wad, a marshmallow, art gum eraser, etc., to serve as a missile. Small, stale marshmallows work well. Metal or other heavy objects could hurt someone or cause damage to things in a room.

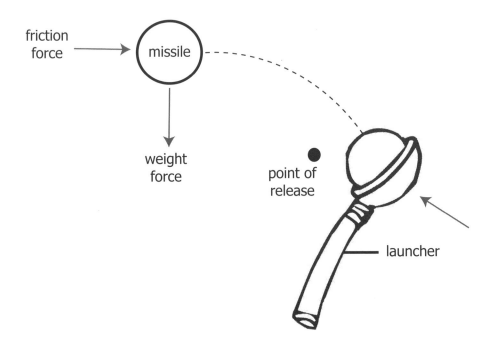

The Science Stuff

The source of energy in this activity is not gravity that pulls down on falling objects. Neither is it a tension force, like that of a bow and arrow. The missile is propelled by a torsion or twisting force. The tighter the rubber band is twisted, the more potential energy it will have. A tightly twisted rubber band can unwind with considerable force.

When the launcher is pulled down and released, the missile goes faster and faster (is accelerated) until it hits the pencil. When the launcher hits the pencil, its motion is stopped suddenly, but the force is transferred to the missile. Even though the launcher stops, the missile doesn't. The missile continues to travel at the same speed and in the same direction until gravity and friction began to affect it (Newton's first law). The faster the launcher accelerates, the more force there will be (Newton's second law).

The launcher continues to accelerate until it is stopped suddenly. When there is not a rigid pencil to stop its movement, the launcher will carry the missile and transfer most of its energy into the table. Unless the missile slips out of the cup during the launch, it will just hit the table forcefully.

The Greek and Roman catapults used heavy rocks as missiles. At first, the rocks would resist starting to move. However, once they were put in motion at a high speed, they would have a tendency to keep on moving straight ahead at the same speed. The moving rocks would resist changing speed and direction.

As the missiles moved through the air, gravity would pull down on them and air friction would push back on them. Eventually they would fall back to the ground. However, they could travel for quite a distance if they were launched with enough force and acceleration.

Making Connections

Aircraft carriers launch their planes by catapults that are built into the ship. These catapults are different in many ways from the ancient Greek and Roman catapults. They are more like a slingshot and use tension forces for launching rather than torsion forces. However, aircraft catapults can launch planes from a short runway on the deck of the ship. These powerful catapults can accelerate a plane from 0 miles/hour to 150 miles/hour in about two seconds. The planes can also land on short runways on another part of the aircraft carrier using special cables and hydraulic equipment.

48

Dig Deeper

Find out more about how the catapults on aircraft carriers work. Make diagrams of them and explain how they work.

The acceleration rate of an airplane that is launched by a catapult is much greater than a car could accelerate. Do a study of the acceleration rates of race cars, planes, rockets, and other devices. Find the world record for acceleration of each device you study. Make a chart or a graph to visually compare these acceleration rates.

Do some research about how pilots are affected by high acceleration rates. NASA has posted a number of pictures of astronauts who are being subjected to high rates of acceleration. You can see how their faces look deformed as the rates increase. These rates are usually referred to as "g forces." What are "g forces"?

Find more information about the ancient Greek and Roman catapults. Include pictures of how they were made. Find out how they were transported to battlefields and how they affected the outcome of wars. Catapults continued to be used as war machines by other countries many years later. What other countries used them?

What Did You Learn?

1. Bow and arrow weapons used tension forces to launch arrows. What kind of force was used by catapults?

2. What can be done to the catapult you built to increase its potential energy?

3. After a missile is launched from a catapult, which of the following will happen: Will the missile's speed continue to get faster and faster or will the missile continue to travel at its same launch speed until other forces cause it to slow down?

4. What is the difference between a tension force and a torsion force?

5. How are planes taking off from an aircraft carrier able to get enough speed to fly?

6. Once a missile has been launched from a catapult and it is moving through the air, what forces begin to act on it to slow it down?

7. Make a diagram of a missile traveling through the air. Use arrows to show the direction of the forces that are causing it to slow down.

8. For an investigation, you constructed and tested a simple catapult. Did the missile accelerate from the time the launcher was released until it hit the pencil?

9. Did the Greeks and Romans design catapults that could be used as war machines before the time of Christ?

49

WHAT DID YOU LEARN?

1. Bow and arrow weapons used tension forces to launch arrows. What kind of force was used by catapults? *Twisting or torsion force.*

2. What can be done to the catapult you built to increase its potential energy? *Twist the rubber band tighter.*

3. After a missile is launched from a catapult, which of the following will happen: Will the missile's speed continue to get faster and faster or will the missile continue to travel at its same launch speed until other forces cause it to slow down? *The second statement.*

4. What is the difference in a tension force and a torsion force? *Tension is the result of pulling or stretching; torsion is the result of twisting.*

5. How are planes taking off from an aircraft carrier able to get enough speed to fly? *They are launched by a catapult that accelerates them in a few seconds to the necessary flying speed.*

6. Once a missile has been launched from a catapult and it is moving through the air, what forces begin to act on it to slow it down? *Gravity pulls down on the missile and friction pushes back on it.*

7. Make a diagram of a missile traveling through the air. Use arrows to show the direction of the forces that are causing it to slow down. *(see page T26)*

8. For an investigation, you constructed and tested a simple catapult. Did the missile accelerate from the time the launcher was released until it hits the pencil? *Yes, the missile accelerates from the time the launcher is released until it hits the pencil. Once it is in the air, its speed will either stay the same or slow down.*

9. Did the Greeks and Romans design catapults that could be used as war machines before the time of Christ? *Yes.*

ISAAC NEWTON

NOTE

This is a good place to point out that many famous scientists were committed Christians who believed the Bible. In fact, before the time of Darwin, most scientists were professing Christians who believed the Bible. Hundreds of pages of Newton's notes about his Bible studies and commentaries are preserved in a museum in Israel. The number of scientists who refer to themselves as atheists or agnostics has greatly increased since Newton's time, especially during the 20th century. However, in recent years, a number of scientists have been willing to challenge Darwin's ideas, even though it has cost some of them their jobs and reputations.

Isaac Newton: A model for a scientist

Isaac Newton is without a doubt one of the world's greatest scientists of all time. His approach to science is a model for scientists everywhere.

Most of us connect Newton's ideas about gravity to a story of him being hit on the head by a falling apple. Newton came to realize that apples and other objects accelerate (fall faster and faster) as they fall. He recognized that gravity was the force causing the apple to accelerate.

The part Newton couldn't figure out was how to do the mathematics of an object that kept on falling faster and faster, because its speed kept changing. The problem of how to deal with the idea of acceleration led him to develop a new kind of math called calculus. Calculus is a valuable tool still used by scientists today.

Newton was able to use mathematics to express all the basic laws he discovered. He opened up vast new areas of research based on his theories of light and his reflecting telescope. He also realized that the laws of motion and gravitation could be applied to the whole universe, not just to things on earth.

Newton was born in 1642, the same year the famous scientist Galileo died. Newton thought much about Galileo's work. He once said that if he had seen farther than others, it was because he had stood on the shoulders of giants. This comment was referring to Galileo and other scientists he had studied.

Galileo was one of the first scientists to believe Aristotle's ideas about forces, motion, and how to study science were wrong. Aristotle arrived at scientific conclusions only by using logic. He thought moving objects stopped moving because they sought a natural state of rest. Galileo's criticism of Aristotle eventually landed him in jail, but Newton was not afraid to agree with Galileo.

Newton used many of Galileo's ideas in writing his three famous laws of motion and his law of universal gravitation. Newton wrote about this in a book called *Principia*. By the end of his life, virtually no reputable scientist thought Newton was wrong about his ideas.

His countrymen considered him the greatest scientist who ever lived. Yet, he spoke freely about his faith in the Bible and his belief in God as the Creator of everything. He believed that eyes and ears could only be the work of a Creator who had great knowledge of optics and sounds.

He noted that the solar system would not work if the speeds of the planets and the mass of the sun were just slightly different. He concluded that the solar system could not be explained by natural causes alone. One of his reasons for studying these things was to show the handiwork of God. Sometimes people think he believed that God created the universe, but then never interacted with it again. This is not what he believed at all.

Newton spent much of his time studying the Bible and writing about it. Remember Newton when you hear criticisms about Christian scientists who believe in the Bible.

50

The following texts reference the contributions of Isaac Newton and other great scientists who saw the hand of the Creator in the wonders of the world. They are all available through Master Books.

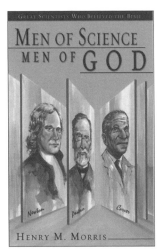

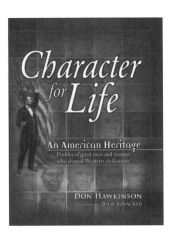

QUIZ ANSWERS:
ANSWERS FOR TRUE AND FALSE QUIZ ABOUT ISAAC NEWTON

1. T	11. F
2. T	12. T
3. F	13. T
4. F	14. T
5. T	15. F
6. T	16. T
7. T	17. F
8. T	
9. T	
10. T	

Learning More about Isaac Newton

There are several good books that have been written about the life of Isaac Newton. Read a book about his life and see if you can determine which five of the following statements are not true.

1. Newton was a Bible scholar who researched the Book of Daniel and spent most of the last year of his life writing about this book.

2. He spent most of his early childhood with his grandmother, because his father died before he was born and his mother remarried.

3. Newton was raised on a large farm by his wealthy father and mother.

4. When Newton first entered school, he was considered the smartest student in school.

5. He was attending school at Cambridge University when the school had to close from 1665 to 1666 because the Plague was causing so many deaths.

6. He was knighted by Queen Anne for his outstanding scientific accomplishments.

7. He invented calculus.

8. He discovered that white light was made up of all the colors of the rainbow. Furthermore, he proposed a theory about the nature of light, and he also designed a reflecting telescope.

9. He formulated the three basic laws of motion.

10. He formulated the law of universal gravitation.

11. He attended Cambridge University where he learned about gravity, light, reflecting telescopes, laws of motion, and calculus.

12. He was president of the Royal Society for many years.

13. He was appointed the Lucasian professor of mathematics at Cambridge.

14. He wrote some famous books about science, especially *Opticks*, and two volumes of *Principia*.

15. He wrote a famous book about the chemistry of farming.

16. He spent much time studying the Bible and left hundreds of pages of handwritten notes about his Bible studies.

17. He was married for 50 years and had 10 children.

Drama Project:
An Interview with Sir Isaac Newton

Use your research on this great scientist to write a series of interview questions, along with the answers, for Isaac Newton as an old man. Get someone to play the role of Isaac Newton. He should dress appropriately to look somewhat like Newton and answer the questions as if he were Isaac Newton. Conduct the interview in front of a group. Keep in mind that he was very intelligent — not weird.

51

DRAMA PROJECT:
AN INTERVIEW WITH SIR ISAAC NEWTON

Finding wigs and authentic-looking clothing may be difficult for many students. An alternative method is to cut a hole in a piece of poster board just big enough for a student's face to fit from chin to forehead. The hair and clothing can be drawn in around the face. A large cardboard box can serve as a support for the poster board or the student can simply hold it in place with his or her hands. Be sure the student acting as Newton uses first person ("I" and "me" instead of "he" or "him"). Remind students that as far as we know, Newton was articulate, polite, and fashionable.

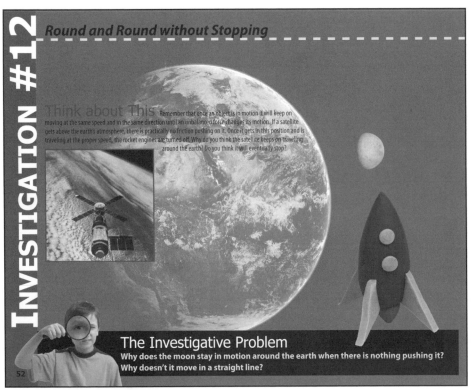

OBJECTIVES

Students use models to help understand that satellites can orbit the earth and the size of their orbits is related to their speed. This is not a perfect model, but it is useful in many ways. Students are reminded that when friction is reduced, a moving object will travel farther before stopping. Building on this and the previous lessons, students should eventually realize that a moving object with no friction could continue to move indefinitely, just as the moon moves around the earth.

NOTE

The equipment for this activity can be adjusted. An empty plastic cylinder from an old ink pen makes a good tube. You may need to cut it so both openings are the same size. Anything about the size and weight of a rubber stopper will work (fishing cork, art gum eraser, etc.), but metal is not advised. This object is going to be spinning around in a big circle. Be sure it will not hurt someone who might accidentally get hit by it. A variety of objects can serve as a small weight; it can be tied or hooked to the string. Be sure to test a model before students use it.

The Science Stuff: Explanations

The stopper is in motion and its inertia causes it to keep traveling at the same speed. It is also trying to go in a straight line because of its inertia. But the force from the string and the weight is constantly pulling on the stopper. This pulling force causes the stopper to go in a circular motion instead of straight. In space, orbits are generally elliptical rather than a perfect circle.

As a model, the plastic tube represents the earth; the weight and the string represent the earth's gravitational pull; and the rubber stopper represents a satellite in orbit around the earth. This is not a perfect model, but it is useful in many ways.

If the speed of an established satellite (or stopper) gets faster, its orbit will get bigger, but it does not require a faster speed to maintain its orbit. If the speed of an established satellite (or stopper) gets slower, its orbit will get smaller. As a satellite goes slower and slower, it will eventually reenter the earth's atmosphere. At this point, the satellite begins to fall and accelerates toward the earth. It reaches extreme speeds as it falls, such that the friction between the satellite and the air produces intense heat. The satellite must be protected by a heat shield or it will burn up. This device could also be used as a model to represent the sun and the earth. The tube would represent the sun; the weight and string, the sun's gravitational pull; and the stopper, the earth.

We will only mention one other thing that can affect the speed of a satellite, but we can't test this. A satellite can be established in orbits thousands of miles from the earth and travel more slowly than it would closer to the earth. For example, at an altitude of 100 miles above the earth, a satellite would need to be traveling 18,000 miles per hour to remain in orbit. At an altitude of 22,300 miles, it can travel at 3,400 miles an hour per hour and remain in orbit. At this speed it would orbit the earth

once every 24 hours. The reason for the different speed requirements is because the earth's gravitational attraction for the satellite continuously gets weaker as it gets farther away from the earth.

Under ordinary conditions on earth, all matter, whether large or small, has weight and takes up space. However, scientists prefer to say that all matter has mass and takes up space. Mass is the amount of matter. The number and kind of atoms in an object would remain the same at sea level, on a mountain, or on the moon. Therefore, the mass would remain the same.

Weight depends on gravitational force. The gravitational force on an object would be less on a mountain than at sea level. It would also be less on the moon than on the earth. For example, if you board an airplane and fly at an elevation of a few miles high, you will lose weight, but your mass will not change.

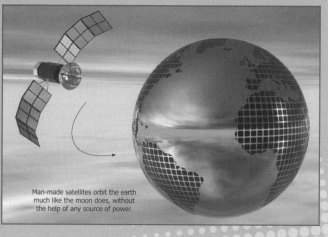

Man-made satellites orbit the earth much like the moon does, without the help of any source of power.

54

Making Connections

Several years ago a space station fell to the earth. It was supposed to last for many years, but what no one had counted on was that the earth's atmosphere unexpectedly expanded. The upper edges of the atmosphere began to rub against the space station as it moved in its orbit around the earth. The friction between the air and the space station caused the station to slow down. Its orbit began to get smaller until it finally crashed and burned. The engineers knew it was probably going to crash, but they didn't have time to do anything about it.

Dig Deeper
Try to find out what kind of man-made satellites and space stations there are in orbit around the earth today. What are their missions?

What Did You Learn?

1. What would happen to an object that was moving at 20 miles per hour if there were no forces acting on it?

2. If the stopper in your model represented the moon, what would the tube represent?

3. In this same model, what would represent the earth's gravitational pull?

4. What would happen if the moon began to slow down? If it began to speed up?

5. Does the size of the earth's orbit around the sun stay the same, get bigger, or get smaller?

6. As the earth orbits the sun, does its speed remain the same, increase, or decrease?

7. What force causes the moon to travel in an orbit around the earth?

8. What happens to a satellite's orbit when it starts to slow down?

9. What would happen to the satellite if its rockets were fired up and made to go faster?

10. Does the earth's gravitational attraction pull as hard on an object in space as it would on that same object at sea level?

11. If you were on the moon, would you weigh the same as you would on earth?

55

WHAT DID YOU LEARN?

1. **What would happen to an object that was moving at 20 miles per hour if there were no forces acting on it?** *It would continue to travel at 20 miles per hour straight ahead.*

2. **If the stopper in your model represented the moon, what would the tube represent?** *The earth.*

3. **In this same model, what would represent the earth's gravitational pull?** *The string and the weight.*

4. **What would happen if the moon began to slow down? If it began to speed up?** *The moon's orbit would get smaller if it slowed down; it would get larger if it sped up.*

5. **Does the size of the earth's orbit around the sun stay the same, get bigger, or get smaller?** *The size of the earth's orbit stays the same.*

6. **As the earth orbits the sun, does its speed remain the same, increase, or decrease?** *The speed of the earth remains the same.*

7. **What force causes the moon to travel in a circular orbit around the earth?** *The earth's gravitational force.*

8. **What happens to a satellite's orbit when it starts to slow down?** *The size of its orbit gets smaller as it slows down.*

9. **What would happen to the satellite if its rockets were fired up and made to go faster?** *The size of its orbit would get larger if its speed increased. (A larger orbit would not require a sustained faster speed.)*

10. **Does the earth's gravitational attraction pull as hard on an object in space as it would on that same object at sea level?** *No, the earth's gravitational attraction gets weaker as the distance from the earth increases.*

11. **If you were on the moon, would you weigh the same as you would on earth?** *No, you would not weigh as much on the moon as you would on earth. (Your mass would not change.)*

Roller Derby with Flour
Action and Reaction

Think about This
Bret and his grandfather went to the firing range. Because Bret had safety training and because his grandfather was there to supervise, Bret was allowed to do some target practice with his grandfather's shotgun. Bret took careful aim and pulled the trigger. Immediately, he was pushed to the ground. What happened?

Safety Note: Even with proper training, never handle firearms without adult permission and constant supervision.

The Investigative Problem
How can a student on a pair of skates illustrate Newton's second and third laws of motion?

56

Gather These Things:
- ✓ Student on roller blades or skates
- ✓ Five-pound bag of flour
- ✓ Metric ruler or tape measure
- ✓ Chalk

Procedure and Observations
The class (or a few demonstration students) will put on roller skates and go outside for this activity. The students should line up in a row facing the instructor. Place a chalk mark where the front wheels are located.

The instructor will hand the first student a five-pound bag of flour.

The student will toss the bag back to the instructor. Describe what happens when the student tosses the bag to the instructor. Place another chalk mark where the front wheels are now located. Measure the distance the student moved. In which direction did the student move?

Repeat with other participating students.

Which student moved back the farthest?

Which student moved back the least amount?

57

OBJECTIVES — Students experience an activity that illustrates action and reaction. Any time there is an action, there will also be an equal and opposite reaction (Newton's third law of motion). This same activity illustrates the relationship between mass and acceleration. If two objects receive the same amount of force, the smaller mass will accelerate more than the larger mass (Newton's second law of motion).

NOTE — This activity is about two of Newton's laws — the second and the third laws of motion. As long as there are examples to visualize, the concepts are not too difficult. They are basic concepts in physical science, but younger students may have trouble keeping the numbers of the laws straight. As a practical guide, try to connect examples with the concepts. Don't be too concerned about the number of the law.

If it seems impractical for an entire class to put on skates, you might want to demonstrate this with a small number of students.

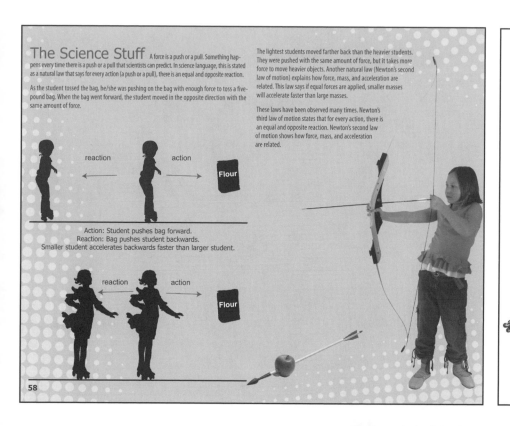

The Science Stuff

A force is a push or a pull. Something happens every time there is a push or a pull that scientists can predict. In science language, this is stated as a natural law that says for every action (a push or a pull), there is an equal and opposite reaction.

As the student tossed the bag, he/she was pushing on the bag with enough force to toss a five-pound bag. When the bag went forward, the student moved in the opposite direction with the same amount of force.

reaction   action

Flour

Action: Student pushes bag forward.
Reaction: Bag pushes student backwards.
Smaller student accelerates backwards faster than larger student.

reaction   action

Flour

The lightest students moved farther back than the heavier students. They were pushed with the same amount of force, but it takes more force to move heavier objects. Another natural law (Newton's second law of motion) explains how force, mass, and acceleration are related. This law says if equal forces are applied, smaller masses will accelerate faster than large masses.

These laws have been observed many times. Newton's third law of motion states that for every action, there is an equal and opposite reaction. Newton's second law of motion shows how force, mass, and acceleration are related.

58

Dig Deeper

1. Find at least five examples that illustrate Newton's second law of motion.

2. Find at least five examples that illustrate Newton's third law of motion.

Making Connections

Have you ever been in a boat and pushed on the dock? Think about what happened. The dock did not move, but your force pushing toward the dock caused you and the boat to move in the opposite direction. This happens because every action has an equal and opposite reaction.

If a 100-pound skater and a 200-pound skater bump into each other while traveling at the same speed, they will both move away from each other. However, the smaller skater will move backward at a faster speed.

What Did You Learn?

1. Newton's third law of motion tells us that every time there is an action, what happens?

2. Refer to the illustration at the beginning of this activity. What caused Bret to be pushed down?

3. What is a likely reason that Bret's grandfather wasn't pushed down when he fired his shotgun?

4. Each student who participated in this activity pitched a five-pound bag of flour to the teacher, but some people moved back more than others. Why was this?

5. Find Newton's third law of motion in a reference book and write it in your own words.

6. We did an investigation where a student exerted a force on a five-pound bag of flour. What did the bag of flour do as a reaction?

59

WHAT DID YOU LEARN?

1. **Newton's third law of motion tells us that every time there is an action, what happens?** *There is an equal and opposite reaction.*

2. **Refer to the illustration at the beginning of this activity. What caused Bret to be pushed down?** *The shotgun pushed on the shots, and the shots pushed on the shotgun. Bret was holding on to the shotgun when it got pushed.*

3. **What is a likely reason for why Bret's grandfather wasn't pushed down when he fired his shotgun?** *Bret's grandfather was probably heavier than Bret. Even though they experienced the same amount of force, the heavier one would move back less than the lighter one.*

4. **Each student who participated in this activity pitched a five-pound bag of flour to the teacher, but some people moved back more than others. Why was this?** *Each student pushed a five-pound bag. The bag pushed back on the students with a five-pound force. According to Newton's second law, if the mass (weight of the student) is big, the acceleration (how fast the student is being pushed back) is small. If the mass is small, the acceleration is big.*

5. **Find Newton's third law of motion in a reference book and write it in your own words.** *Whenever one object exerts a force on another object, the second one exerts an equal and opposite force on the first one.*

6. **We did an investigation where a student exerted a force on a five-pound bag of flour. What did the bag of flour do as a reaction?** *The bag of flour pushed back on the student with an equal force.*

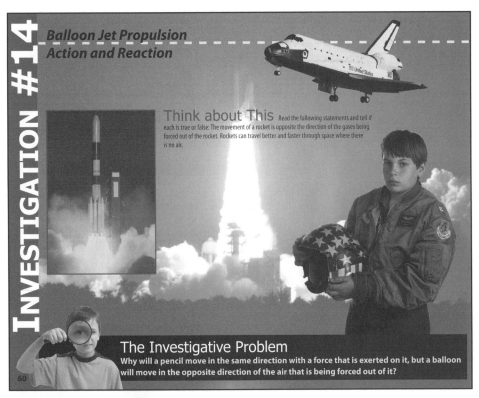

Balloon Jet Propulsion
Action and Reaction

Think about This
Read the following statements and tell if each is true or false: The movement of a rocket is opposite the direction of the gases being forced out of the rocket. Rockets can travel better and faster through space where there is no air.

The Investigative Problem
Why will a pencil move in the same direction with a force that is exerted on it, but a balloon will move in the opposite direction of the air that is being forced out of it?

60

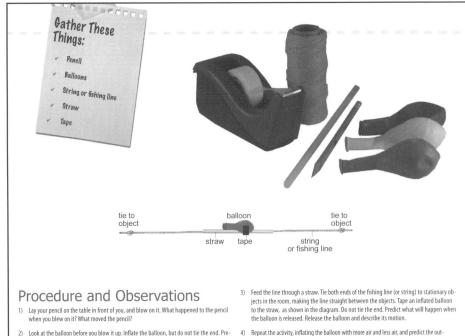

Gather These Things:
- ✓ Pencil
- ✓ Balloons
- ✓ String or fishing line
- ✓ Straw
- ✓ Tape

tie to object — balloon — tie to object

straw   tape   string or fishing line

Procedure and Observations

1) Lay your pencil on the table in front of you, and blow on it. What happened to the pencil when you blew on it? What moved the pencil?

2) Look at the balloon before you blow it up. Inflate the balloon, but do not tie the end. Predict what will happen when you let go of the balloon. Release the balloon and see what happens.

3) Feed the line through a straw. Tie both ends of the fishing line (or string) to stationary objects in the room, making the line straight between the objects. Tape an inflated balloon to the straw, as shown in the diagram. Do not tie the end. Predict what will happen when the balloon is released. Release the balloon and describe its motion.

4) Repeat the activity, inflating the balloon with more air and less air, and predict the outcomes.

61

OBJECTIVES

Students observe another action-reaction where a blown-up balloon pushes on the air inside, while this same air pushes back on the balloon.

NOTE

Read the following statements and ask the student to tell if he or she thinks each is true or false:

1. The movement of a rocket is opposite the direction of the gases being forced out of the rocket.

2. Rockets can travel better and faster through space where there is no air.

Both statements are true. Give the students an opportunity to think about whether they are true. Then give them the correct answers without further explanations until after they complete the activity.

unbalanced force   unbalanced force

An unbalanced force (wind) will cause a pencil to accelerate more than a heavier can.

The Science Stuff
The wind was an unbalanced force on the pencil. The pencil started moving because an unbalanced force was applied to it. The greater the force of the wind on the pencil, the faster the pencil moved and accelerated. If you blow forcefully on both a pencil (a small mass) and a heavier cylindrical object (a larger mass), the small mass accelerates faster than the large mass. Newton's second law of motion, which you studied in the previous lesson, explains the behavior of the pencils and the can. Newton's third law of motion explains the behavior of the balloon.

When the balloon was released initially, it flew in every direction. The balloon moved in a straight line on the string, because an additional force was added that held it straight.

When air is released from the balloon, the elasticity of the balloon acts as a force on the air inside the balloon, forcing it out. Newton's third law of motion explains what happened. The air being forced out the back of the balloon pushes back on the balloon with an equal and opposite force. While the escaping air goes backward, the balloon goes forward. Another way to state what happened is to say for every action, there is an equal and opposite reaction.

Balloon moves opposite from escaping gases   Elastic forces push air out of balloon

Air is forced out of the balloon in one direction,
Balloon moves in the opposite direction.
Action: Balloon pushes air.
Reaction: Air pushes balloon.

escaping gases

62

Making Connections
Rockets have an advantage over airplanes, because rockets are not limited to the air. Rockets work in the air, but they also work above the air in space. In fact, they work more efficiently in space. Airplanes can only fly where there is air.

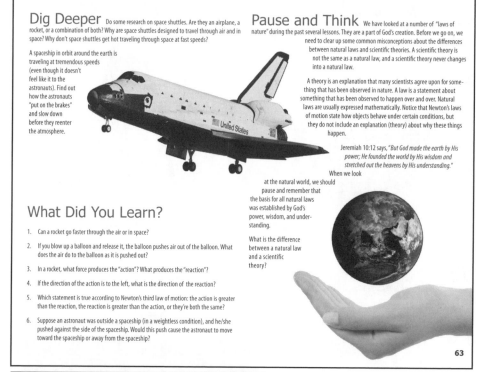

Dig Deeper
Do some research on space shuttles. Are they an airplane, a rocket, or a combination of both? Why are space shuttles designed to travel through air and in space? Why don't space shuttles get hot traveling through space at fast speeds?

A spaceship in orbit around the earth is traveling at tremendous speeds (even though it doesn't feel like it to the astronauts). Find out how the astronauts "put on the brakes" and slow down before they reenter the atmosphere.

United States

What Did You Learn?

1. Can a rocket go faster through the air or in space?

2. If you blow up a balloon and release it, the balloon pushes air out of the balloon. What does the air do to the balloon as it is pushed out?

3. In a rocket, what force produces the "action"? What produces the "reaction"?

4. If the direction of the action is to the left, what is the direction of the reaction?

5. Which statement is true according to Newton's third law of motion: the action is greater than the reaction, the reaction is greater than the action, or they're both the same?

6. Suppose an astronaut was outside a spaceship (in a weightless condition), and he/she pushed against the side of the spaceship. Would this push cause the astronaut to move toward the spaceship or away from the spaceship?

Pause and Think
We have looked at a number of "laws of nature" during the past several lessons. They are a part of God's creation. Before we go on, we need to clear up some common misconceptions about the differences between natural laws and scientific theories. A scientific theory is not the same as a natural law, and a scientific theory never changes into a natural law.

A theory is an explanation that many scientists agree upon for something that has been observed in nature. A law is a statement about something that has been observed to happen over and over. Natural laws are usually expressed mathematically. Notice that Newton's laws of motion state how objects behave under certain conditions, but they do not include an explanation (theory) about why these things happen.

Jeremiah 10:12 says, "But God made the earth by His power; He founded the world by His wisdom and stretched out the heavens by His understanding." When we look at the natural world, we should pause and remember that the basis for all natural laws was established by God's power, wisdom, and understanding.

What is the difference between a natural law and a scientific theory?

63

WHAT DID YOU LEARN?

1. **Can a rocket go faster through the air or in space?** *A rocket can travel faster through space, because there is no air resistance or friction to slow it down.*

2. **If you blow up a balloon and release it, the balloon pushes air out of the balloon. What does the air do to the balloon as it is pushed out?** *The air pushes back on the balloon.*

3. **In a rocket, what force produces the "action"? What produces the "reaction"?** *Action: the rocket pushes gases out. Reaction: the gases push back on the rocket.*

4. **If the direction of the action is to the left, what is the direction of the reaction?** *To the right.*

5. **Which statement is true according to Newton's third law of motion: the action is greater than the reaction, the reaction is greater than the action, or they're both the same?** *The same, because they're equal and opposite.*

6. **Suppose an astronaut was outside a space ship (in a weightless condition), and he/she pushed against the side of the spaceship. Would this push cause the astronaut to move toward the space ship or away from the spaceship?** *Away. (The spaceship would also be pushed, but its much greater mass would cause negligible movement back.)*

PAUSE AND THINK

Early peoples were tempted to credit idols with various acts of creation and often worshiped and offered sacrifices to the sun, the moon, animals, or other beings. God repeatedly warned His people to worship Him and no others. There was no place for compromise in dealing with idolatry. God is justified in bringing judgment on those who put their trust and faith in worthless idols and teach others to do this, too.

Balancing Act with a Stick
Center of Gravity and Mass

Think about This The lady who walked across the tightrope holding a long pole fascinated Grace when she went to the circus with her parents. Grace thought the lady could walk easier if she would put the pole down, but her dad laughed and said she would fall if she didn't hold the pole. This made no sense to Grace, because she had not yet learned about the center of gravity.

Since 1922, the Flying Wallendas has been the name of a famous group of circus act and daredevil stunts performers, most known for performing death-defying stunts without a safety net.

The Investigative Problem
What is the center of gravity of an object? How can you balance a popsicle stick vertically on the end of your fingertip?

64

Gather These Things:
- ✓ Popsicle stick (or something similar)
- ✓ Four to six metal washers or nuts
- ✓ Ruler
- ✓ Single strand insulated wire, 30 cm long
- ✓ Sharpened pencil

Procedure and Observations
Hold your pencil horizontal to the floor and lay it across your finger, moving it until it is balanced. The place where it balances is the center of gravity of the pencil.

Try balancing a popsicle stick vertically on the tip of your finger, not across. Can you do it?

Follow these instructions to construct a balancing stick that will balance on the tip of your finger. From one end of the popsicle stick, measure about 3 cm and mark that point. Bend the wire in half to find the middle and wrap it around the stick twice at the mark. The two wire ends should be the same length. Pull the wires down toward the short end of the stick. Bend the ends of the wire to form hooks. Add a washer or nut to each hook. You may need to bend the hook over the weight.

Try to balance the stick on the tip of your finger. If it falls over, notice which way it fell. Make a slight adjustment by bending the wires up or down. Notice how your adjustment affects the balance and keep trying. It may take a little patience to get the stick to balance.

Try adding more washers or nuts to the wire hooks. Does adding more weights make it easier or harder for you to balance the stick vertically?

65

OBJECTIVES Students learn how to find the center of gravity of an object. They observe that changing an object's mass at certain positions can change its center of gravity.

NOTE Before doing the activity, spend some time discussing circus tightrope performers and the purpose of the long pole they carry. Ask the students if they think the pole helps them balance better or if it makes it harder for them to balance. Challenge the students to figure out how to make a popsicle stick balance vertically on their finger. Assure them there is a way to do it.

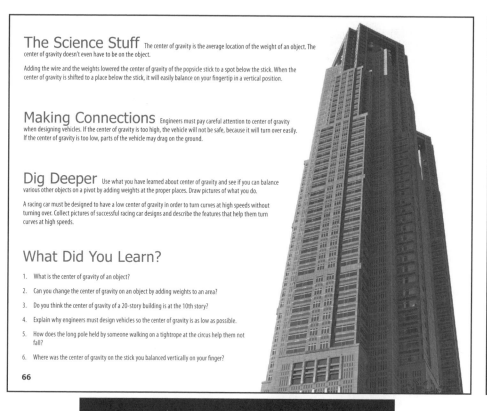

The Science Stuff
The center of gravity is the average location of the weight of an object. The center of gravity doesn't even have to be on the object.

Adding the wire and the weights lowered the center of gravity of the popsicle stick to a spot below the stick. When the center of gravity is shifted to a place below the stick, it will easily balance on your fingertip in a vertical position.

Making Connections
Engineers must pay careful attention to center of gravity when designing vehicles. If the center of gravity is too high, the vehicle will not be safe, because it will turn over easily. If the center of gravity is too low, parts of the vehicle may drag on the ground.

Dig Deeper
Use what you have learned about center of gravity and see if you can balance various other objects on a pivot by adding weights at the proper places. Draw pictures of what you do.

A racing car must be designed to have a low center of gravity in order to turn curves at high speeds without turning over. Collect pictures of successful racing car designs and describe the features that help them turn curves at high speeds.

What Did You Learn?

1. What is the center of gravity of an object?
2. Can you change the center of gravity on an object by adding weights to an area?
3. Do you think the center of gravity of a 20-story building is at the 10th story?
4. Explain why engineers must design vehicles so the center of gravity is as low as possible.
5. How does the long pole held by someone walking on a tightrope at the circus help them not fall?
6. Where was the center of gravity on the stick you balanced vertically on your finger?

66

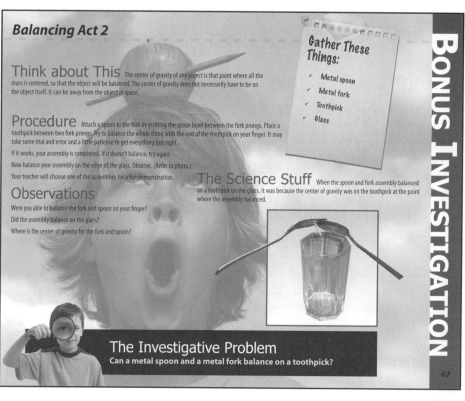

Balancing Act 2

Think about This
The center of gravity of any object is that point where all the mass is centered, so that the object will be balanced. The center of gravity does not necessarily have to be on the object itself. It can be away from the object in space.

Procedure
Attach a spoon to the fork by pushing the spoon bowl between the fork prongs. Place a toothpick between two fork prongs. Try to balance the whole thing with the end of the toothpick on your finger. It may take some trial and error and a little patience to get everything just right.

If it works, your assembly is completed. If it doesn't balance, try again.

Now balance your assembly on the edge of the glass. Observe. (Refer to photo.)

Your teacher will choose one of the assemblies for a fun demonstration.

Observations
Were you able to balance the fork and spoon on your finger?

Did the assembly balance on the glass?

Where is the center of gravity for the fork and spoon?

The Science Stuff
When the spoon and fork assembly balanced on a toothpick on the glass, it was because the center of gravity was on the toothpick at the point where the assembly balanced.

Gather These Things:
- ✓ Metal spoon
- ✓ Metal fork
- ✓ Toothpick
- ✓ Glass

The Investigative Problem
Can a metal spoon and a metal fork balance on a toothpick?

67

BONUS INVESTIGATION

WHAT DID YOU LEARN?

1. **What is the center of gravity of an object?** *The average location of the weight of an object.*

2. **Can you change the center of gravity on an object by adding weights to an area?** *Yes.*

3. **Do you think the center of gravity of a 20-story building is at the 10th story?** *No, it is much lower than that.*

4. **Explain why engineers must design vehicles so the center of gravity is as low as possible.** *If the center of gravity is too high, the vehicle might turn over too easily.*

5. **How does the long pole held by someone walking on a tightrope at the circus help them not fall?** *The weight, shape, and position of the pole lowers the person's center of gravity, which makes it easier to maintain balance.*

6. **Where was the center of gravity on the stick you balanced vertically on your finger?** *It was below the stick.*

Spinning Tops
Rotational Inertia and Mass

Think about This

Observe the teacher demonstration if a suitable swivel chair is available. Have a student sit in a swivel chair with his or her legs pulled up to the seat and crossed. Then follow these instructions. Hold two heavy books close to body. While the chair is spinning, hold one book in each hand and extend arms in opposite directions. As the chair continues to spin, bring the books back close to body. Continue to alternately hold books out at arm's length and bring them in close. Observe how the speed changes as the position of the books is changed.

If a swivel chair is not available, discuss how an ice skater can slow his or her rotational speed by extending both arms and one leg. Discuss how rotational speed can be increased by bringing arms close to body and holding legs together.

The humble spinning top has been a children's favorite for literally thousands of years, with variations on the theme first appearing around 2000 BC.

Procedure and Observations

Part A

We have seen how the speed of a rotating object can be changed. In this part of the investigation, we will look at how mass can affect the time a rotating object continues to spin.

The Investigative Problem

Can you balance a toy top when it is not moving? Can you balance a toy top when it is moving? How does the mass of a spinning top affect its motion?

68

Gather These Things:

- ✓ Pencil or a small dowel rod
- ✓ 10-cm diameter circular disc cut from cardboard or poster board (with every 60 degrees marked)
- ✓ Timer or watch with second hand
- ✓ Six paper clips (same size)
- ✓ Six pennies
- ✓ Tape
- ✓ Scissors

1) Place the pointed end of the pencil down on a smooth surface, such as glass. Try spinning the pencil by itself. It may take you a little while to get the technique of spinning the pencil. One method is to put the pencil between your thumb and middle finger and make a snapping motion. Another method is to put the pencil between both hands, with fingers extended. Move one hand forward and the other hand backwards at the same time. Remember that the pencil will not always spin, even though your technique is good. Could the pencil by itself spin very well? (Since this may leave pencil marks on the table, you may want to tape a smooth piece of paper down first or use a small wooden dowel.)

2) Cut out a circular disc (10 cm diameter) from a piece of heavy cardboard or poster board if your teacher did not provide this. Divide the disc into six equal sections. If the sections are equal, they will all be 60-degree angles.

3) Poke the pencil through the center of the cardboard disc. Bring the disc down until it is about 3 or 4 cm from the pointed end of the pencil. If the pencil is not securely in place, try wrapping some tape around the pencil or just tape the pencil to the disc.

4) Try to spin the pencil now. What happened this time?

5) Spin your top three times and record how long it spins each time before falling over.

6) Add mass to the top by placing a paper clip over each line on the circle. Spin your top three times and record how long it spins. Is it harder to get the top started spinning with the paper clips?

7) Place a penny under each paper clip, sliding the penny as close to the edge as you can.

8) Spin the top three times. After every spin, record the time it continues to spin. Was it harder or easier to get the spinning started with the added mass?

69

OBJECTIVES

Students investigate variables that affect the length of time a spinning top can continue to balance and spin.

NOTE

This is an interesting demonstration provided you have a swivel chair and a cooperative student. If you chose to do this demonstration, do a practice session first. Have a student sit in a swivel chair with his or her legs pulled up to the seat and crossed. Give him or her a stack of books to hold in his or her lap. Now spin the chair. While the chair is spinning, have the student alternately hold the books out at arm's length and bring them in close. Observe how the speed changes as the position of the books are changed.

If a swivel chair is not available, lead a discussion about the spins conducted during figure skating competitions. Ice skaters can spin around very fast when they hold their arms close to their bodies. They spin slower when they hold their arms out.

Collect a variety of materials for Part B, such as cardboard, poster board, scissors, tape, glue, paper plates, Styrofoam plates, old CD discs, pennies, paper clips, and pencils or other cylindrical objects. Encourage students to be creative and to test and modify their spinning tops to make them spin longer. This could generate even more interest if done as a contest with prizes for the winner.

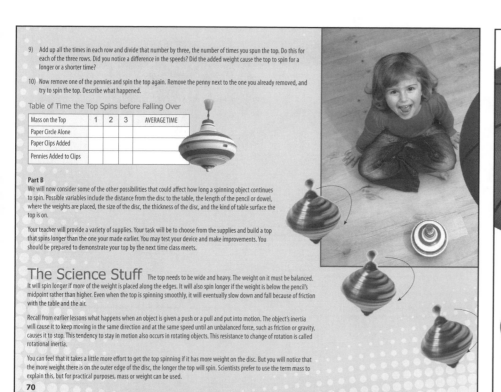

9) Add up all the times in each row and divide that number by three, the number of times you spun the top. Do this for each of the three rows. Did you notice a difference in the speeds? Did the added weight cause the top to spin for a longer or a shorter time?

10) Now remove one of the pennies and spin the top again. Remove the penny next to the one you already removed, and try to spin the top. Describe what happened.

Table of Time the Top Spins before Falling Over

Mass on the Top	1	2	3	AVERAGE TIME
Paper Circle Alone				
Paper Clips Added				
Pennies Added to Clips				

Part B

We will now consider some of the other possibilities that could affect how long a spinning object continues to spin. Possible variables include the distance from the disc to the table, the length of the pencil or dowel, where the weights are placed, the size of the disc, the thickness of the disc, and the kind of table surface the top is on.

Your teacher will provide a variety of supplies. Your task will be to choose from the supplies and build a top that spins longer than the one your made earlier. You may test your device and make improvements. You should be prepared to demonstrate your top by the next time class meets.

The Science Stuff

The top needs to be wide and heavy. The weight on it must be balanced. It will spin longer if more of the weight is placed along the edges. It will also spin longer if the weight is below the pencil's midpoint rather than higher. Even when the top is spinning smoothly, it will eventually slow down and fall because of friction with the table and the air.

Recall from earlier lessons what happens when an object is given a push or a pull and put into motion. The object's inertia will cause it to keep moving in the same direction and at the same speed until an unbalanced force, such as friction or gravity, causes it to stop. This tendency to stay in motion also occurs in rotating objects. This resistance to change of rotation is called rotational inertia.

You can feel that it takes a little more effort to get the top spinning if it has more weight on the disc. But you will notice that the more weight there is on the outer edge of the disc, the longer the top will spin. Scientists prefer to use the term mass to explain this, but for practical purposes, mass or weight can be used.

70

Making Connections

When a large ceiling fan is turned off, it may continue to turn for a few minutes. Large, heavy fans that are well-balanced and lubricated are most likely to keep turning. If you see a ceiling fan that is wobbly, its weight is probably not balanced. Flat pieces of metal can be taped to the upper sides of the blades to adjust for uneven weight. Does this seem to be related to the center of gravity?

Dig Deeper

Do planets and moons rotate at constant velocities? Are there any factors that might cause their velocities to eventually change?

Try to collect a variety of spinning tops. See which ones are able to spin for the longest time. How does the size, shape, and weights of these tops compare to the ones you designed that have short spinning times? How do they compare to the ones you designed that have long spinning times? Can you make adjustments on them to make them spin longer?

Pause and Think

When a circular object is rotating, the motion will be smooth if the center of gravity is located where the object is rotating. It will be wobbly if there is more weight on one side than on the other. The same thing is true of spherical rotating objects, like the earth, the moon, and the planets. The moon causes the earth to have a slight wobble, but the earth itself is amazingly balanced.

Isaiah 40:12 recognizes God's wisdom and power in creating weight balance on earth and in the heavens: "Who has measured the waters in the hollow of his hand, or with the breadth of his hand marked off the heavens? Who has held the dust of the earth in a basket, or weighed the mountains on the scales and the hills in a balance?"

Once, when Job thought God had treated him unfairly, God reminded Job that he did not have the ability to understand some things. This is what God said to Job: "Where were you when I laid the earth's foundation? Tell me, if you understand. Who marked off its dimensions? Surely you know. Who stretched a measuring line across it? On what were its footings set, or who laid its cornerstone" (Job 38:4–6).

David often marveled at God's creation and praised God for setting the moon and the stars in the heavens while they moved in predictable ways: "When I consider your heavens, the work of your fingers, the moon and the stars, which you have set in place, what is man that you are mindful of him" (Psalm 8:3–4).

We should be just as amazed as Job, Isaiah, and David at God's unlimited understanding, power, and wisdom in creating everything with such precision and balance.

What Did You Learn?

Write in your own words some of the main ideas you learned from doing this activity.

71

WHAT DID YOU LEARN?

Write in your own words some of the main ideas you learned from doing this activity. *Keep this open-ended. Students will probably notice that the top is harder to start, but will spin longer with more weights. The weights should be a distance away from the pencil and located below the mid point of the pencil. Encourage students to include some of the things they learned as the built their own spinning tops.*

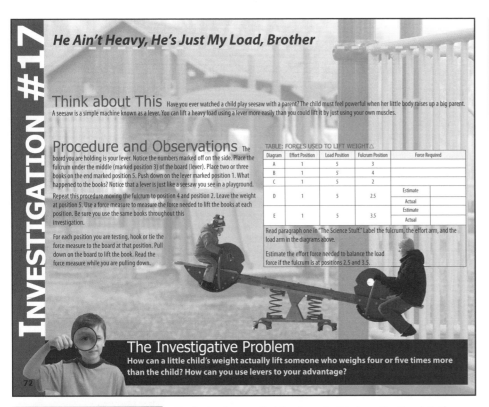

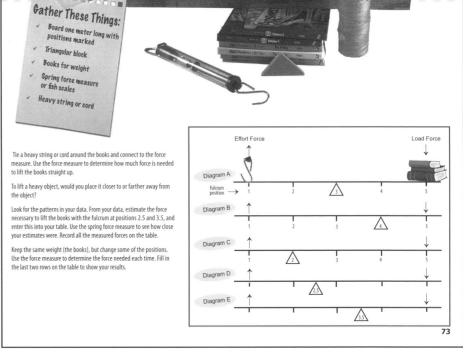

INVESTIGATION #17

He Ain't Heavy, He's Just My Load, Brother

Think about This Have you ever watched a child play seesaw with a parent? The child must feel powerful when her little body raises up a big parent. A seesaw is a simple machine known as a lever. You can lift a heavy load using a lever more easily than you could lift it by just using your own muscles.

Procedure and Observations
The board you are holding is your lever. Notice the numbers marked off on the side. Place the fulcrum under the middle (marked position 3) of the board (lever). Place two or three books on the end marked position 5. Push down on the lever marked position 1. What happened to the books? Notice that a lever is just like a seesaw you see in a playground.

Repeat this procedure moving the fulcrum to position 4 and position 2. Leave the weight at position 5. Use a force measure to measure the force needed to lift the books at each position. Be sure you use the same books throughout this investigation.

For each position you are testing, hook or tie the force measure to the board at that position. Pull down on the board to lift the book. Read the force measure while you are pulling down.

TABLE: FORCES USED TO LIFT WEIGHT△

Diagram	Effort Position	Load Position	Fulcrum Position	Force Required
A	1	5	3	
B	1	5	4	
C	1	5	2	
D	1	5	2.5	Estimate
				Actual
E	1	5	3.5	Estimate
				Actual

Read paragraph one in "The Science Stuff." Label the fulcrum, the effort arm, and the load arm in the diagrams above.

Estimate the effort force needed to balance the load force if the fulcrum is at positions 2.5 and 3.5.

The Investigative Problem
How can a little child's weight actually lift someone who weighs four or five times more than the child? How can you use levers to your advantage?

72

Gather These Things:
- Board one meter long with positions marked
- Triangular block
- Books for weight
- Spring force measure or fish scales
- Heavy string or cord

Tie a heavy string or cord around the books and connect to the force measure. Use the force measure to determine how much force is needed to lift the books straight up.

To lift a heavy object, would you place it closer to or farther away from the object?

Look for the patterns in your data. From your data, estimate the force necessary to lift the books with the fulcrum at positions 2.5 and 3.5, and enter this into your table. Use the spring force measure to see how close your estimates were. Record all the measured forces on the table.

Keep the same weight (the books), but change some of the positions. Use the force measure to determine the force needed each time. Fill in the last two rows on the table to show your results.

73

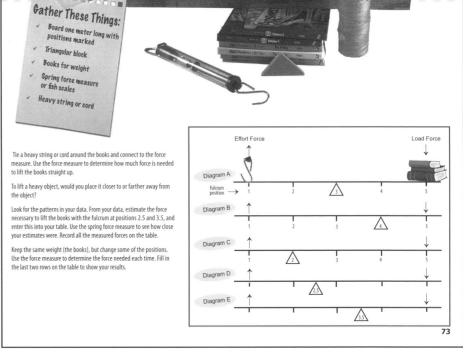

OBJECTIVES

Students observe that the lever in this investigation lets them apply a smaller force than the machine exerts. At the same time, the input force moves through a greater distance than the machine's output force.

NOTE

Obtain a board that is a little longer than 80 cm in length, leaving a few cm at each end to support the books. Mark every 20 cm, and label the marked positions as 1, 2, 3, 4, and 5. Help students recall what they know about a seesaw. Put a fulcrum under the board and balance a heavy object with a light object. For more clarity, designate an object that needs to be lifted to be the load. Identify the fulcrum, the effort force, the load force, the effort arm, and the load arm.

The Science Stuff

The fulcrum divides a first-class lever into two parts, called the "effort arm" and the "load arm." The load arm is the distance from the fulcrum to where the load rests. The effort arm is the distance from the fulcrum to where you apply your effort force.

In a first-class lever, the fulcrum is between the effort and the load, and it changes the direction of the load; that is, you move the load up by pressing down on the opposite end. There are other "classes" of levers. All levers have a fulcrum, an effort arm, and a load arm. In second, and third-class levers, the fulcrum is on the end of the lever.

If you divide the length of the effort arm by the length of the load arm, you get a number that tells you how many times the lever will multiply your effort force. This is called the mechanical advantage. In diagram A, if the effort arm is 4 meters and the load arm is 2 meters, the mechanical advantage will be 2. Therefore, a 6 pound effort force will lift a 12 pound load.

In diagram B, the load would be easier to lift (but slower) if it were moved closer to the fulcrum. The load will move farther (but will be harder to move) if it is moved away from the fulcrum. Diagram B shows 2 variations of levers. Notice the effort force pulls up rather than pushing down in each. Notice the fulcrum is on the end in each case rather than being between the effort and the load.

With a first-class lever, moving the fulcrum closer to the weight makes it easier to lift the weight. But the trade-off is in speed and the distance you can lift the load. Your hand moves a long distance while the weight moves a short distance. As an example, a crowbar can help you pry open a stuck window that you can't move at all with your hands. While the window moves a few centimeters, your hand will probably move 30 or 40 centimeters.

The farther away the fulcrum is from the weight (load), the harder it is to lift, so more effort is needed. The advantage of this kind of lever is that the effort force only moves a small distance while the load force moves a long distance. The load also moves faster. For example, a fly swatter moves faster than your hand could move. The advantage is that you hit the fly faster, not harder.

Levers are so common in our everyday lives that we may not realize how often we use them. Bottle openers, shovels, brooms, scissors, fishing poles, your arms, and your legs are examples of different kinds of levers.

Class 1 Lever — Effort, Load, Fulcrum or Pivot Point **A**

Class 2 Lever — Load, Fulcrum or Pivot Point, Effort

Class 3 Lever — Load, Fulcrum or Pivot Point, Effort **B**

Making Connections

If you use a simple cane fishing pole to lift a five-pound fish from the water, you will have to exert much more than five pounds of effort force in the process. The advantage of using a fishing pole is that the fish will move a long distance at the same time your hand moves a short distance. The effort force (your hand) is close to the fulcrum, and the load (the fish) is a long distance from the fulcrum.

A bottle opener is also a lever. The fulcrum is very close to the load and far away from the effort force. With a bottle opener, a small effort force can move a very large resistance. However, the bottle cap only moves a short distance.

effort force / load

Dig Deeper

Draw pictures of a fly swatter, a baseball bat, a wheelbarrow (the wheel is only to reduce friction), and a bottle opener. See if you can show where your effort force would be applied and where the machine (the lever) would apply a force.

Try to list at least 20 other machines that are levers. Second-class and third-class levers are variations in the locations of the fulcrum, effort force, load force, and in the direction the load moves. Include all kinds of levers. Tell if the lever mainly makes it easier to move something or lets you move something faster than your hand moves. Some machines just change the direction of the force.

Try to construct a lever with a mechanical advantage of at least 10 that will let you lift a 10-pound weight using 1 pound or less of effort force.

74

Project — Human Machines

(Count as two projects)

Your arms and your legs are levers. Start with your arm, and draw a picture of it. Find a good reference book to help you with your drawing. Identify the effort force (provided by the biceps muscle), the load lever arm, a weight held in the hand (the load force), and the fulcrum (at the elbow). Notice where the muscles and tendons are attached to the bones. If you are able to locate all the places where forces are applied, you should be able to see that this is a third-class lever.

The effort force comes from your biceps muscle. The muscle contracts and gets shorter. It may make a "bulge" at the same time. When the muscle contracts, it pulls on the tendon that connects to a bone in the lower arm. This raises the lower arm. To lower the arm, the triceps muscle contracts and pulls the arm back down.

What Did You Learn?

1. To lift a heavy object, would you place the fulcrum close to or farther away from the object?

2. In a lever, a rigid bar rotates around a fixed point. What is the fixed point in a lever?

3. In a first-class lever, where is the fulcrum?

4. Is the advantage of using a fly swatter to hit the fly faster or harder?

5. Give an example of a lever that lets you move a very heavy object a short distance.

6. Give an example of a lever that lets you move an object much faster than your hand is moving.

7. An effort lever arm is 4 meters long and the load lever arm is 1 meter long. What is the mechanical advantage of the lever?

The science part is interesting. Compare the force exerted by your biceps muscle to a weight you are lifting. In your drawing, show the distance from the elbow to where the biceps muscle connects to the lower arm bone. This is the effort lever arm. Measure the distance from the elbow to the hand. This is the load lever arm. You will find that the load lever arm is longer than the effort lever arm. This means the force of your muscles must be greater than the force of the weight. (Theoretically, the force of your biceps muscle times the effort lever arm equals the weight of your lower arm and hand, plus whatever your hand is holding multiplied by the load lever arm.)

Now consider the advantages of this design. If your hands were closer to your elbows, the load lever arm would be shorter and you could lift heavier weights. You might like the idea of being able to lift heavy weights, but there would be a disadvantage to this design. If your arms were shorter, you would lose the advantage of moving your arm through a longer distance. Imagine how hard it would be to get food to your mouth or comb your hair if your hands were near your elbows! Your muscle only moves about a centimeter as it contracts, but your arm moves many centimeters when this happens. What problems would there be if your arms were longer?

Sometimes evolutionists say they don't believe God created living things because they think they have observed things that are not well designed. Do you think your arm is well designed? Do you believe you could have designed it better than God did?

Sometimes evolutionists say that similarities of arms and legs in other animals prove that all animals have a common ancestor. Find out what creation scientists have to say about this. Creatively display what you have learned and share with your class. You may also want to include information about your legs, which are also levers.

75

PROJECT — HUMAN MACHINES

Even if students don't choose to do this project, take time to introduce the following ideas. The lever in the previous lesson was a first-class lever. This project involves a third-class lever, but the basic terminology is the same. This will be an opportunity for a more in-depth investigation of a machine.

Evolutionists like to note that many animals, including fish, birds, and land animals, have similar patterns of one bone attached to the body, which is attached to two bones, which are attached to many bones. This allows vastly more freedom of movement than two bones attached to a body, which are attached to one bone.

Some scientists argue that there are only a few ways that bones can fit together and still work well. They don't consider similarities of bone patterns a strong argument for a common ancestor. There is an excellent discussion of this in *Explore Evolution*, written by Stephen C. Meyer, Scott Minnich, Jonathan Moneymaker, Paul A. Nelson and Ralph Seelke (Melbourne & London: Hillhouse Publishers TM, 2007).

For grading purposes, count this as two projects.

WHAT DID YOU LEARN?

1. To lift a heavy object, would you place the fulcrum close to or farther away from the object? *Closer to the fulcrum*.

2. In a lever, a rigid bar rotates around a fixed point. What is the fixed point in a lever? *The fulcrum.*

3. In a first-class lever, where is the fulcrum? *Somewhere between the effort force and the load force.*

4. Is the advantage of using a fly swatter to hit the fly faster or harder? *To hit the fly faster.*

5. Give an example of a lever that lets you move a very heavy object a short distance. *Crowbar, car jack, bottle opener, (others).*

6. Give an example of a lever that lets you move an object much faster than your hand is moving. *Baseball bat, golf club, fly swatter, (others).*

7. An effort lever arm is 4 meters long and the load lever arm is 1 meter long. What is the mechanical advantage of the lever? *4 divided by 1 = 4, so the mechanical advantage of the lever is 4.*

How Do Like Your Pulleys — Fixed, Moving, or Combined?

Think About This

There was a big discussion about how to move Aunt Martha's expensive antique piano from her second floor apartment. It weighed 800 pounds and would have to go down a flight of stairs to get to the loading truck. Everyone wondered how Aunt Martha ever got it up there in the first place. Just as Cousin Eric started to push it toward the stairs, Cousin Jackson said, "Wait. There's an easier way. We can lower it from the window with a block and tackle." What could Jackson's idea be for two men to lower an 800-pound piano from a second story building?

Procedure and Observations

Part A. Fixed Pulley

Push the wire through the hole in the spool. Bring the ends together, twist several times, and put the wires over a support. Weigh the load (bucket and weight inside) and record. Tie the cord to the handle of the bucket and bring the cord over the spool. Tie the other end of the cord to the force measure (spring scale). Pull down on the force measure to lift the weight. Be sure to pull straight down and not to the side. Pull steadily on the force measure to lift the load about 30 cm and record the following:

1) Direction the load bucket and weight moved as the effort (your hand) moved downward.
2) Distance traveled by the effort (your hand) as the load moved 30 cm.
3) Amount of force required to lift the load using a fixed pulley.
4) Record weight of the load (bucket and weight).

Did the pulley make it easier for you to lift the load?

Did the pulley cause the load to move more or less than the distance your hand had to move?

Did the pulley cause the load to move in the opposite direction from the way your hand moved?

Compare the weight of the load (bucket and weight) to the effort force needed to lift the load using a fixed pulley.

100 N 100 N 100 N 100 N

The Investigative Problem
What is a fixed pulley? What is a moving pulley? What is a combination pulley system?

76

Gather These Things:
- Two large empty thread spools
- Small bucket with handle containing a weight (load)
- Spring force measure
- Heavy cord
- Measuring stick or tape measure
- 30 cm solid core insulated wire

Part B. Movable Pulley

Now disconnect the spool and wire pulley. Tie one end of the cord to a support. Hold the spool and wire pulley with the wire turned down. Connect the bucket and weight to the ends of the wire. Slide the cord under the spool and tie the other end of the cord to the force measure.

Estimate the amount of force that will be needed to lift the bucket and weight using a movable pulley. Lift the bucket and weight by pulling up on the force measure. Lift the bucket and weight a distance of 30 cm. Record the following information:

1) Direction the load (bucket and weight) moved as the effort force (your hand) moved upward.
2) Distance traveled by the effort force (your hand) as the load moved 30 cm.

0 N 50 N

100 N

3) Amount of force required to lift the load using a movable pulley.
4) Amount of force required to lift the load without using a pulley.

Estimate the distance the load will travel as your hands move 20 cm. Now try it and record the actual distance your hands moved.

Did the movable pulley make it easier for you to lift the load?

Did the pulley cause the load to move more or less than the distance your hand had to move?

Did the pulley cause the load to move in the opposite direction from the way your hand had to move?

Compare the weight of the load (bucket and weight) to the effort force needed to lift the load using a movable pulley.

77

OBJECTIVES Students investigate a fixed pulley and a movable pulley. Their advantages and disadvantages are compared. Systems that combined both fixed and movable pulleys are considered.

NOTE If you have regular pulleys and clamps to support them, you may prefer to use this equipment. Either way, be sure students thoroughly investigate a single fixed pulley and a single movable pulley before combining them. The terminology and concepts about machines are probably new to many students. Be sure they have correct answers to the "What Did You Learn?" questions.

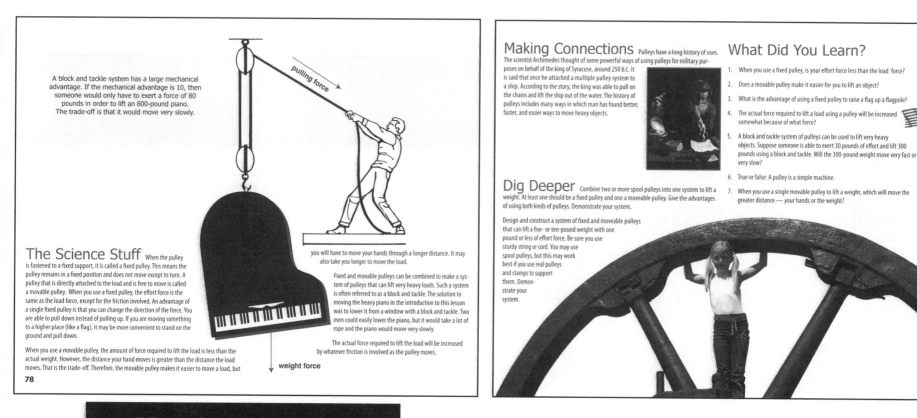

A block and tackle system has a large mechanical advantage. If the mechanical advantage is 10, then someone would only have to exert a force of 80 pounds in order to lift an 800-pound piano. The trade-off is that it would move very slowly.

pulling force

The Science Stuff

When the pulley is fastened to a fixed support, it is called a fixed pulley. This means the pulley remains in a fixed position and does not move except to turn. A pulley that is directly attached to the load and is free to move is called a movable pulley. When you use a fixed pulley, the effort force is the same as the load force, except for the friction involved. An advantage of a single fixed pulley is that you can change the direction of the force. You are able to pull down instead of pulling up. If you are moving something to a higher place (like a flag), it may be more convenient to stand on the ground and pull down.

When you use a movable pulley, the amount of force required to lift the load is less than the actual weight. However, the distance your hand moves is greater than the distance the load moves. That is the trade-off. Therefore, the movable pulley makes it easier to move a load, but you will have to move your hands through a longer distance. It may also take you longer to move the load.

Fixed and movable pulleys can be combined to make a system of pulleys that can lift very heavy loads. Such a system is often referred to as a block and tackle. The solution to moving the heavy piano in the introduction to this lesson was to lower it from a window with a block and tackle. Two men could easily lower the piano, but it would take a lot of rope and the piano would move very slowly.

The actual force required to lift the load will be increased by whatever friction is involved as the pulley moves.

weight force

78

Making Connections

Pulleys have a long history of uses. The scientist Archimedes thought of some powerful ways of using pulleys for military purposes on behalf of the king of Syracuse, around 250 B.C. It is said that once he attached a multiple pulley system to a ship. According to the story, the king was able to pull on the chains and lift the ship out of the water. The history of pulleys includes many ways in which man has found better, faster, and easier ways to move heavy objects.

Dig Deeper

Combine two or more spool pulleys into one system to lift a weight. At least one should be a fixed pulley and one a moveable pulley. Give the advantages of using both kinds of pulleys. Demonstrate your system.

Design and construct a system of fixed and moveable pulleys that can lift a five- or ten-pound weight with one pound or less of effort force. Be sure you use sturdy string or cord. You may use spool pulleys, but this may work best if you use real pulleys and clamps to support them. Demonstrate your system.

What Did You Learn?

1. When you use a fixed pulley, is your effort force less than the load force?

2. Does a movable pulley make it easier for you to lift an object?

3. What is the advantage of using a fixed pulley to raise a flag up a flagpole?

4. The actual force required to lift a load using a pulley will be increased somewhat because of what force?

5. A block and tackle system of pulleys can be used to lift very heavy objects. Suppose someone is able to exert 30 pounds of effort and lift 300 pounds using a block and tackle. Will the 300-pound weight move very fast or very slow?

6. True or false: A pulley is a simple machine.

7. When you use a single movable pulley to lift a weight, which will move the greater distance — your hands or the weight?

79

WHAT DID YOU LEARN?

1. When you use a fixed pulley, is your effort force less than the load force? *No.*

2. Does a movable pulley make it easier for you to lift an object? *Yes.*

3. What is the advantage of using a fixed pulley to raise a flag up a flagpole? *Your force can pull down on the flagpole rope and make the flag move up the pole.*

4. The actual force required to lift a load using a fixed pulley will be increased somewhat because of what force? *Friction.*

5. A block and tackle system of pulleys can be used to lift very heavy objects. Suppose someone is able to exert 30 pounds of effort and lift 300 pounds using a block and tackle. Will the 300-pound weight move very fast or very slow? *Very slow.*

6. True or false: A pulley is a simple machine. *True.*

7. When you use a single movable pulley to lift a weight, which will move the greater distance — your hands or the weight? *Your hands.*

And the Wheel Goes Round

Think about This

The doorknob came off the door to Mr. Livingston's classroom as the class was ready to leave for the day. It wouldn't go back on because the connector was broken. Everyone tried to turn the little rod that was supposed to connect to the knob, but the door wouldn't open. Even the strongest person in class couldn't make it turn enough to open the door. Finally, Mary Charles said she had an idea. She took her hair barrette and pushed it through a hole in the rod. Holding the hair barrette, the rod turned easily and the door opened. What was her secret?

Harry Houdini was a Hungarian American magician and escapologist. Early in his life, Houdini mastered the ability to pick locks, thus opening the door to a career as an escape artist. He forever changed the world of magic and escapes.

Procedure and Observations

Observe how a screwdriver acts as a wheel and axle by turning a metal screw into a scrap piece of wood. Compare a screwdriver with a big diameter handle (wheel) to a screwdriver with a small handle (wheel). Record your observations about how much effort force each one took to turn the screw into the wood.

Make a windlass type of wheel and axle as follows. Push a pencil through the hole in the empty sewing spool. Add glue to the pencil if the pencil slips in the spool. Hammer a thin nail through the metal holder for the eraser to make a hole. Remove the nail. Straighten a paper clip and push it through the hole in the eraser. Bend the paper clip in the shape of a crank. Bend the other end to keep it from sliding out.

Turn the board so that the hook screws are pointing toward the floor or parallel to the floor. Place the pencil through the round openings, as in the diagram. Place a small clamp to the end of the pencil to keep it from sliding out of the hooks. Secure one end of the string to the spool and wrap the string around the spool several times.

The Investigative Problem

Does a wheel and axle move things faster or easier?

80

Gather These Things:

- ✓ A large empty sewing spool
- ✓ Pencil with an eraser
- ✓ A weight
- ✓ Large paper clip
- ✓ Heavy string
- ✓ Small handle flathead screwdriver
- ✓ Big handle flathead screwdriver
- ✓ Flathead metal screws (same size)
- ✓ Board with two hook screws (used for Activity #11)
- ✓ C-clamp if needed to hold board to table
- ✓ Scrap wood for screws

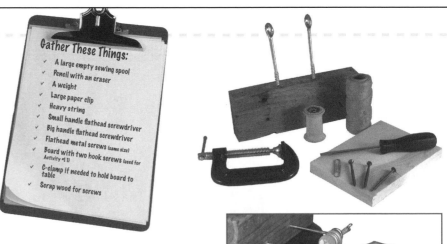

Attach the weight to the end of the string and lower the weight to the floor. Turn the crank to lift it. Notice how fast it moves and how easy it is to lift it. Count the number of times the crank must turn to lift the weight to the table.

Now move the string so that it rolls up on the pencil instead of on the spool. Lower the weight to the floor and turn the crank. Compare how fast it moves and how easy it is to lift to the previous test. Count the number of times the crank must turn to lift the weight to the table.

You have just constructed two wheel and axles. Notice that your hand makes a big circle as it turns the paper clip crank. The turning crank is the wheel part. Whatever the string winds up on is the axle part. You used a large axle the first time and a small axle the second time.

Pull directly on the cord to lift the weight, and compare these results with the previous tests.

81

OBJECTIVES

Students investigate another kind of simple machine — a wheel and axle. They observe that a force applied to the wheel will cause the axle to exert a bigger force. They also observe that a force applied to the axle will make a wheel move much faster.

NOTE

Students may incorrectly think that skate wheels are the same as a wheel and axle machine. Be sure to point out that in a wheel and axle machine, the wheel turns as the axle turns and the axle turns as the wheel turns. In skate wheels, the axle is stationary and only the wheel turns. The equipment you used in lesson #11 can be modified to use in this activity.

The Science Stuff

The wheel and axle is really one machine with two parts that are firmly attached to each other. You can calculate how much the machine will multiply your force (its mechanical advantage) by dividing the diameter of the wheel by the diameter of the axle. MA = DW/DA.

To use a screwdriver, your hand turned the wheel (the handle). The wheel turned the axle, and the axle turned the screw. Your hand must make many turns in order to cause the screw to move down into the wood a short distance. The larger the wheel, the less your effort force must be.

With the windlass, the same principle applies. The wheel does not have to be a complete wheel in order to be considered a wheel and axle. It can be just a crank. The crank acts like a wheel when it makes a complete circle.

If the diameter of the axle (the drum) is four cm and the diameter of the wheel (the crank) is 40 cm, the windlass should be able to multiply your force ten times. The mechanical advantage of this machine would be ten. Although friction would reduce the advantage somewhat, you could lift a 30-pound bucket with about three pounds of effort force. You would also have to turn the crank ten times longer. If you make the axle (the drum) larger, it would take more effort force to lift the bucket of water, but you could do it faster and with less turning.

In some devices, a force is applied to the axle, causing the wheel to turn. You have to use a big force to turn an axle, but the advantage is that the wheel moves very fast. This is the principle of an electric fan, where the motor turns the axle and the axle turns the fan blades.

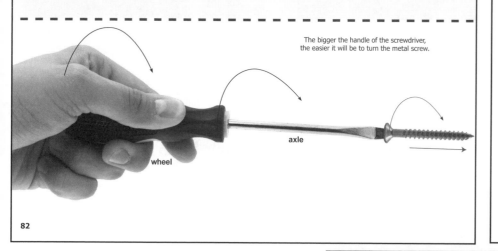

The bigger the handle of the screwdriver, the easier it will be to turn the metal screw.

wheel

axle

82

Making Connections

Other examples of crank-wheels are pencil sharpeners and winches on a boat trailer.

Look at an outdoor water faucet. How hard would it be to turn the faucet if all you had to hold onto was the little rod that came out of the center?

Sometimes it is an advantage to apply a force to the axle, because that will cause the wheel to turn very fast. Gear systems in bicycles allow the rider to make decisions about what kind of advantage is needed.

Bicycles used by professional riders, such as the ones used in the Tour de France, have about 20 different gears. This helps them in a variety of situations, such as climbing up steep mountain roads, riding through low hills, or traveling on level roads.

Dig Deeper

Obtain a set of gears. You may be able to find a set of plastic toy gears. Count the "teeth" in each. Connect a small gear to a big gear, and count the number of times a small gear turns while a big gear turns once. Turn a small gear and observe what a large gear does at the same time. Try different arrangements. Keep a chart of your results. Look for patterns in your numbers.

Imagine that you were a farmer living 100 years ago. You have just constructed a well, and you need to build a windlass to pull up water from the well in a bucket. Assume a bucket of water weighs 30 pounds and the well is 30 feet deep. Think about the observations you made from the windlass models. Decide if you would make the drum (the axle) large or small. Having a small drum would make it easier to lift the bucket of water, but having a large drum would let you lift the bucket faster. There is an advantage both ways. However, you can't have the full advantage of both at the same time. You might want to lift something that weighs 30 pounds to see how heavy a bucket of water would feel. Calculate the mechanical advantage of different windlasses. When you have this information, decide how you would build your windlass.

What Did You Learn?

1. True or false: A wheel and axle is one simple machine.

2. It would be easier to lift a bucket of water using which kind of windlass — a big crank (the wheel) and a small axle (the drum) or a big crank and a big axle?

3. Which kind of windlass would allow you to lift a bucket of water faster — a big crank and a small axle or a big crank and a big axle?

4. What kind of screwdriver would you choose if you needed to turn a big metal screw into a piece of wood?

5. What kind of screwdriver would you choose if you needed to replace a small screw in a pair of eyeglasses?

6. Why are the wheels on a pair of skates not part of a wheel and axle simple machine? Is this the same as a wheel and axle simple machine?

7. In cars and trucks, the steering wheel is attached to an axle. Is this an example of a wheel and axle simple machine?

8. If the diameter of a crank (the wheel) in a windlass measures 50 cm and the diameter of the drum (the axle) measures 10 cm, what is the mechanical advantage of this wheel and axle machine?

9. How much force would it take for you to lift 100 pounds using the machine described in question #8 (not counting friction)?

10. Draw a picture of a screwdriver and identify the wheel and the axle.

83

WHAT DID YOU LEARN?

1. True or false: A wheel and axle is one simple machine. *True*.

2. It would be easier to lift a bucket of water using which kind of windlass — a big crank (the wheel) and a small axle (the drum) or a big crank and a big axle? *A big crank and a small axle would provide the easiest way to lift a bucket of water.*

3. Which kind of windlass would allow you to lift a bucket of water faster — a big crank and a small axle or a big crank and a big axle? *A big crank and a big axle would allow you to lift the bucket of water faster (but it would take more effort force to lift).*

4. What kind of screwdriver would you choose if you needed to turn a big metal screw into a piece of wood? *A heavy-duty screwdriver with a big handle.*

5. What kind of screwdriver would you choose if you needed to replace a small screw in a pair of eyeglasses? *A small screwdriver with a thin handle.*

6. Why are the wheels on a pair of skates not part of a wheel and axle simple machine? Is this the same as a wheel and axle simple machine? *The wheels on a pair of skates turn around a stationary axle. In a wheel and axle machine, the wheel and axle is one unit that turns together.*

7. In cars and trucks, the steering wheel is attached to an axle. Is this an example of a wheel and axle simple machine? *Yes, when the wheel turns, the axle also turns. (The axle connects to some gears.)*

8. If the diameter of a crank (the wheel) in a windlass measures 50 cm and the diameter of the drum (the axle) measures 10 cm, what is the mechanical advantage of this wheel and axle machine? *The mechanical advantage of the wheel and axle machine is 5 (50cm divided by 10cm = 5).*

9. How much force would it take for you to lift 100 pounds using the machine described in question #8 (not counting friction)? *If the mechanical advantage is 5, that means your effort force will be multiplied by 5 times. Think: 5 times what number will equal 100? The answer is 20 pounds.*

10. Draw a picture of a screwdriver and identify the wheel and the axle. *Picture of screwdriver with wheel and axle labeled.*

If It Doesn't Move, How Can It Be a Machine?

Think about This

Marty was wet with sweat after an hour at work on his new job. His assignment for the day was to load stacks of 50-pound boxes onto the delivery truck. After an hour of work, he still had 35 boxes to go. He looked up to see his girlfriend Maria standing by the truck.

"Do you want to know an easier way to do this?" she asked sweetly.

Marty hated to admit it, but she was usually right about everything. Looking at the 35 boxes waiting to be loaded, he said, "Sure. What's your great idea?"

"First of all, put up the loading ramp. Second, slide the boxes onto the little roller carts. That way, you will be using a simple machine that will make it easier to move the boxes. The roller carts will also make it easier and in addition will reduce friction," Maria replied. She had always wanted to put her knowledge of science to use. Now was a good time to see if all the science stuff really worked.

Marty was proud of his athletic abilities and strength, but this was more than he had bargained for. He was amazed as he rolled the next box up the ramp. "This is much easier than lifting a fifty-pound box straight up from the ground. All it costs me is to push the boxes a little farther. Did you really learn this in a science class?"

The Investigative Problem
Is it easier to lift a heavy object by pulling it up a ramp or by picking it straight up? How can wedges and screws be simple machines? How can a screw, a wedge, and an inclined plane be related?

84

Gather These Things:

- ✓ Flat board about 40 cm long for a ramp
- ✓ Spring force measure
- ✓ Object to move (about five pounds)
- ✓ Stack of books
- ✓ Paper
- ✓ Pencil
- ✓ Scissors
- ✓ Black marker
- ✓ Flathead screwdriver
- ✓ Scrap wood pieces
- ✓ Various kinds of flathead metal screws of same length

Procedure and Observations

Place one end of the flat board on a stack of books to make a ramp. Slide an object (approximately five pounds) up the ramp. Use a spring force measure to see how much force this takes. Lift the object straight up while using a force measure. Record both forces.

Now draw a diagonal from one corner to the other on a sheet of paper. Cut along the line to make a triangle. With the black marker, make a heavy black line along the longest side of the triangle. Look at this and see how it compares to an inclined plane.

Wrap the paper triangle around a pencil so that the heavy black line in the triangle resembles the threads on the screw. How do the threads of the screw compare to an inclined plane?

Choose three different kinds of metal screws. Use a screwdriver and screw each one into a piece of scrap wood. Be sure to use the same screwdriver each time and be sure each screw is the same length. Rank the screws from easiest to hardest to turn. Observe each of the screws. Notice how far apart the grooves are and other differences in the screws. Record this information.

Look at a wedge. How does it resemble an inclined plane?

85

OBJECTIVES

Students investigate three other simple machines — inclined planes, screws, and wedges. Inclined planes don't move as they are being used. Screws and wedges are very similar to inclined planes, but they do move as they are being used. They have the advantage of making it easier to move something. The disadvantage is that the distance over which the force must move is increased.

NOTE

This is the last lesson about machines. This would be a good time to reinforce that a **simple machine** can do one of three things. It can multiply your force; it can multiply the distance your force moves (or move something faster); or it can change the direction of your force. If a simple machine multiplies your force, it cannot multiply the distance through which you move a force at the same time. Sometimes a simple machine is only used to change the direction of a force. A compound machine is made up of more than one simple machine and can be designed for different purposes.

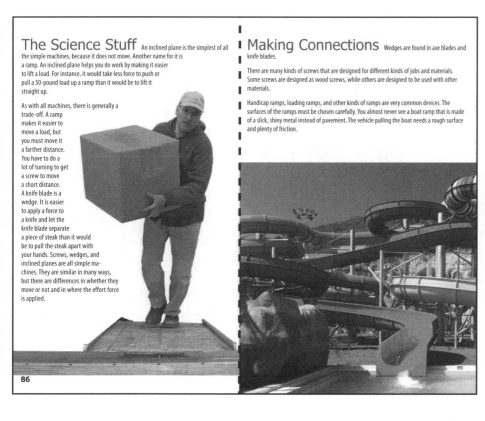

The Science Stuff
An inclined plane is the simplest of all the simple machines, because it does not move. Another name for it is a ramp. An inclined plane helps you do work by making it easier to lift a load. For instance, it would take less force to push or pull a 50-pound load up a ramp than it would be to lift it straight up.

As with all machines, there is generally a trade-off. A ramp makes it easier to move a load, but you must move it a farther distance. You have to do a lot of turning to get a screw to move a short distance, because it does not move. A screw is a wedge. It is easier to apply a force to a knife and let the knife blade separate a piece of steak than it would be to pull the steak apart with your hands. Screws, wedges, and inclined planes are all simple machines. They are similar in many ways, but there are differences in whether they move or not and in where the effort force is applied.

Making Connections
Wedges are found in axe blades and knife blades.

There are many kinds of screws that are designed for different kinds of jobs and materials. Some screws are designed as wood screws, while others are designed to be used with other materials.

Handicap ramps, loading ramps, and other kinds of ramps are very common devices. The surfaces of the ramps must be chosen carefully. You almost never see a boat ramp that is made of a slick, shiny metal instead of pavement. The vehicle pulling the boat needs a rough surface and plenty of friction.

86

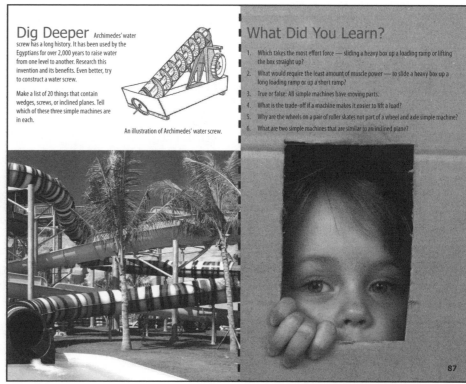

Dig Deeper
Archimedes' water screw has a long history. It has been used by the Egyptians for over 2,000 years to raise water from one level to another. Research this invention and its benefits. Even better, try to construct a water screw.

Make a list of 20 things that contain wedges, screws, or inclined planes. Tell which of these three simple machines are in each.

An illustration of Archimedes' water screw.

What Did You Learn?
1. Which takes the most effort force — sliding a heavy box up a loading ramp or lifting the box straight up?
2. What would require the least amount of muscle power — to slide a heavy box up a long loading ramp or up a short ramp?
3. True or false: All simple machines have moving parts.
4. What is the trade-off if a machine makes it easier to lift a load?
5. Why are the wheels on a pair of roller skates not part of a wheel and axle simple machine?
6. What are two simple machines that are similar to an inclined plane?

87

WHAT DID YOU LEARN?

1. **Which takes the most effort force — sliding a heavy box up a loading ramp or lifting the box straight up?** *You would move a greater distance in sliding a heavy box up a loading ramp than in lifting it straight up from the ground.*

2. **What would require the least amount of muscle power — to slide a heavy box up a long loading ramp or up a short ramp?** *It would take less muscle power to slide a heavy box up a long loading ramp than up a short ramp.*

3. **True or false: All simple machines have moving parts.** *False.*

4. **What is the trade-off if a machine makes it easier to lift a load?** *You (or the effort force) must move a greater distance compared to not using the machine.*

5. **Why are the wheels on a pair of roller skates not part of a wheel and axle simple machine?** *In a wheel and axle machine, the wheel and the axle are attached together so that when one turns, the other turns. In roller skates, only the wheels turn; the axle doesn't turn.*

6. **What are two simple machines that are similar to an inclined plane?** *Wedge and screw.*

An exciting 3rd to 6th grade science curriculum!

Finally, a way to study science that your kids will love. Learn science basics like physics and chemistry while you have lots of fun with this activity-based series. Includes activities related to:

- friction
- speed
- inertia
- speed
- lift
- mass
- weight
- gravity
- energy
- force
- density

Important scientific terms and concepts are introduced in an engaging series of investigative lessons. Designed to fit into any education program, this informative series offers the best in science education and biblical reinforcment.

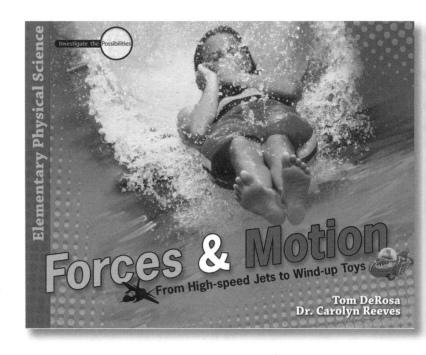

11 x 8.5 • Perfect Bound • Full Color • 88 pages
Retail: $12.99 U.S.
ISBN-13: 978-0-89051-539-6

11 x 8.5 • Perfect Bound • Full Color • 96 pages
Retail: $12.99 U.S.
ISBN-13: 978-0-89051-560-0

Forces and Motion - Teacher's Guide
11 x 8.5 • Paperback • 48 pages
Retail: $4.99 U.S.
ISBN-13: 978-0-89051-541-9

Matter - Teacher's Guide
11 x 8.5 • Paperback • 48 pages
Retail: $4.99 U.S.
ISBN-13: 978-0-89051-561-7

Forces and Motion - Student Journal
11 x 8.5 • Paperback • 48 pages
Retail: $4.99 U.S.
ISBN-13: 978-0-89051-540-2

Matter - Student Journal
11 x 8.5 • Paperback • 48 pages
Retail: $4.99 U.S.
ISBN-13: 978-0-89051-559-4